COPYWRITING
FOR MARKETING
COMMUNICATIONS

Ashley Hastings

CGW PUBLISHING

2019

Copywriting for Marketing Communications

First Edition   November 2019

ISBN 978-1-9082934-5-9

CGW Publishing 2019

CGW Publishing

B1502

PO Box 15113

Birmingham

B2 2NJ

www.cgwpublishing.com

mail@cgwpublishing.com

About the Author

Ashley Hastings has been putting the ideas described in this book into practice for over 20 years. Through his own copywriting business, he has helped companies of all sizes and from all sectors communicate their marketing message to the people that matter.

www.ashleyhastings.co.uk

To Susan, Mabel, Evie and Arthur

CONTENTS

INTRODUCTION

A blueprint for assembling great copy

Hello

WHAT'S THE POINT OF THIS BOOK?

It is a fact that most people can write and, with the help of modern technology, create a presentable piece of marketing communications free from spelling mistakes and with all the apostrophes in the right place. But will it strike a chord with its target audience? Will its message leap from the page and capture the reader's imagination? Will it convey a clear compelling idea with instantaneous impact? No, it won't.

To create something with more appeal than an office memo, marketing material requires more than just writing. It requires copywriting. And, with so much competing content to go up against, it takes exceptional copywriting to cut through the noise and inspire action from the reader.

A skilled marketing communications copywriter has the ability to craft content that engages and motivates readers with all the clarity and conviction of a personal invitation from the Archangel Gabriel.

This book will give you these skills.

What's so good about this book?

Copywriting for Marketing Communications covers every stage of the copywriting process. It explains how to get your head round the purpose of a particular piece of marketing material and how to get into the head of the intended recipient. It shows you how to plan to achieve your objective, strike the right tone and summon up the creative magic that transforms dull, lifeless text into an irresistible proposition that sparkles with clarity and demands attention.

You don't need to read the whole book to acquire this knowledge. Each chapter is a self-contained masterclass covering a particular form of marketing material. So you can explore the chapters in whatever order you like (but read the *Don't do anything until you have read this* chapter first).

Every step of every method is tackled with meticulous attention to detail. Nothing is glossed over, but nothing is included unless it is strictly relevant to the task at hand. The result is a clear, comprehensive and enjoyable-to-read handbook for anyone wishing to produce expertly crafted marketing communications.

What makes this book different from the rest?

If you are taking a sneaky peak at this book while standing in a bookshop or browsing online, having a free read to see if it's worth forking out for, you will notice there are a few similar books available to purchase. To help you make your decision, here is what this book is not:

- *◊* It is not a general marketing book, so it doesn't say things like "leverage your customer base," whatever that means.

- *◊* It is not a book that teaches you to trick customers with hype, spin and misinformation.

- *◊* It is not a book that offers superficial platitudes such as 'your headline should be catchy' without giving you the slightest clue how to actually accomplish it.

Instead, *Copywriting for Marketing Communications* is about skilfully bridging the gap between writer and recipient in a way that resonates with the reader and evokes a genuine interest. It is filled with strategies you can understand and clear demonstrations of what works – all described in simple, engaging language.

Depending on your individual circumstances, *Copywriting for Marketing Communications* can be a student textbook, a handy DIY manual or an authoritative source of reference. So, whether you're an existing copywriter, an absolute beginner, someone who writes copy as part of a wider role or a manager responsible for reviewing the work of a marketing team, this book will give you the expert insight you need to improve your skills and gain an in-depth understanding of marketing communications copywriting.

In the following pages you will find knowledge, know-how, tips, techniques, secrets and assorted sorcery distilled into simple building blocks along with clear instructions on how to deploy them for maximum effect. Which is exactly how you should approach your marketing communications copywriting.

As legendary copywriter Eugene Schwartz said: "You do not write copy, you assemble it." In which case, treat this book as your blueprint.

Oh, and one last thing. As some of you will be aspiring freelance copywriters or possibly part of a marketing team in a large corporation or maybe something in-between, I use the term 'your business' throughout the book to refer to the organisation you are writing for – whoever that may be.

Thank you for your time. Have fun, and let me know how you get on.

DON'T DO ANYTHING UNTIL YOU HAVE READ THIS

Avoid common crimes against readability

Words are powerful things and they need to be handled with care. Elegantly tailored to suit their purpose, the right words will demand attention, capture the imagination and bring your communications to life.

Bear the contents of this section in mind before you begin writing and use it as a checklist when you have finished – and soon you will be deploying words that couldn't have more impact if they had a nuclear warhead attached to them.

WHAT'S IN THIS CHAPTER?

❶ MAXIMISING READABILITY

Just one flaw in your otherwise splendid piece of marketing communications can make you look like a bungling amateur who can't string a sentence together.

Here are some tips to ensure your message is conveyed with the utmost correctness and clarity.

Spelling

If you struggle with spelling or get muddled with 'there' and 'their', there are plenty of simple guides to be found on the web as well as the spelling and grammar checker within Microsoft Word.

Grammar

To a great extent, marketing communications use spoken English rather than grammatically perfect English. So not knowing a split infinitive from a dangling participle is unlikely to detract from the meaning of your message. Even so, the fundamentals need to be correct – such as where your apostrophes are positioned – otherwise the entire meaning can be altered. If unsure, check one of the numerous websites dedicated to this subject.

Focus

Remove anything that is not relevant to the point you are trying to convey. Any unnecessary clutter will cause the reader to lose interest. As the French writer, Antoine de Saint-Exupéry, put it: "A designer knows he has achieved perfection, not when there is nothing left to add, but when there is nothing left to take away."

Simplicity

Replace jargon and complex language with simple words. Imagine it has to be understood by a 12 year old. That's about the level of clarity you need to be aiming for.

Sentences

Use short, punchy sentences rather than long, clumsy ones. Short sentences are simpler to read, easier to understand and give your language a natural rhythm.

Words

Make every word count. Any redundant words should be cut. For example: 'The new design is bright red in colour' should be 'The new design is bright red'.

Descriptions

When describing something, bring it to life in the reader's mind. For example: 'It is a big table' should be 'The table is roomy enough to seat 8 people comfortably'.

Gaffes

Look out for words that at first seem correct, but actually are not. For example: 'I could of danced all night' should be 'I could have danced all night'.

Errors

The temptation is to skim over commonly used but essential information, such as contact details. As a result, errors easily slip through. Check them a hundred times. Then get someone else to check them.

❷ MINIMISING MISTAKES

The following suggestions will help to prevent errors occurring in the first place and make it easier for you to achieve the outcome described in the previous checklist.

Make the most of Word

Microsoft Word's editing and correction features are far superior to those of most other applications. Where specialist software is needed, such as WordPress for blogs, it is best to carry out your work in Word before transferring the text to the specialist application.

Write first, edit later

It's easier to get something down on paper then pull it into shape than stare at a blank page until your head bleeds, agonising over what the first word should be.

Forget about it

When you have finished writing your piece of marketing communications, take a break. Go away and do something else. Preferably leave it overnight. Then come back to it with a fresh mind. Now you can approach it more like someone reading it for the first time.

Get someone else to check it

It often takes a detached viewpoint to spot a glaring error. Let someone not involved with your business take a look at what you have written, as if from the customers' point of view. Ask them to play Devil's advocate and go through it with a fine toothed comb, scribble on it, point out any boring or confusing bits and identify where they feel information is lacking.

ADVERTORIALS

Write articles with the
commercial clout of an advert

After much research involving monkeys and copies of Reader's Digest, it is a proven fact that a published article interlaced with sales information will be read by far more people and generate far more responses than a straightforward advertisement.

This hybrid of journalism and marketing is the advertorial – a blend of the words 'advertisement' and 'editorial'. All it takes to write one is a little journalistic know-how, or should that be journo-how?

WHAT'S IN THIS CHAPTER?

❶ STEALTH ADVERTISING

A successful advertorial looks like a genuine news story, reads like a genuine news story, and has the editorial credibility of a genuine news story – but is written by you to impart sales information to prospective customers.

Although it lurks, chameleon-like, among the regular content of a publication, it is not an unscrupulous attempt to deceive the hapless reader. An advertorial is a factual news story – it just sells by not selling.

What's it about?

The whole idea behind the advertorial is that it looks and sounds like an editorial. So, the subject of your advertorial has got to be news of some sort. By 'news' I don't mean a dramatic event (don't get carried away, you are not a real journalist), I mean an issue that will be of interest to your intended reader. And that ain't your business or even what your business does.

Resist the urge to bang on about the business. If the most compelling story you have to tell is "We have been in business for 15 years" or "We offer exceptional customer service", readers will not only turn the page, they will actively dislike the business for being so boring and wasting their time.

Any reference to products and services must form a natural part of a meaningful news story. Don't attempt to mutate a piece of blatant promotion into an interesting story. It doesn't work. The story must incorporate the marketing message, not the other way round.

The piece must fit in seamlessly with the publication's usual content. Otherwise, it will look as phoney as one of those awful TV adverts with a serious looking 'news reporter' telling you about the great value underlay at Carpet Kingdom.

Taking these points into account, acceptable subjects for an advertorial fall into two distinct camps.

The two possible themes for an advertorial
1. A problem facing the reader (that your business can solve)
2. An event (involving your business) that will interest the reader

These general themes can be applied to advertorials relating to any product or service, whether you are addressing the public or other businesses.

Here are some examples of a problem facing the reader (that your business can help solve)...

- Cybercrime (IT consultant)

- Furnishing your home on a budget (furniture retailer)

- How to live with poor vision (optician)

- Dirty facilities in restaurants (manufacturer of a hygiene monitor)

- Keeping kids active in winter (pre-school nursery)

- A survey showing that 28% of drivers can't park properly (driving instructor)

And here are some examples of an event (involving your business) that will interest the reader...

- A classic car on display in the foyer of your premises (vehicle customisation business)

- The revamp of local landmark building (a business that has moved into the well-known location)

- An exciting new beauty treatment (beauty salon)

- Mums-to-be get a free relaxing shoulder massage (maternity shop)

- A local start-up business fair (business consultant)

- A new show at the local theatre (clothes designer who designed the costumes)

Where will it appear?

An advertorial is not written then dispatched to dozens of different publications (like a press release). It is a one-off, written for a single, specific publication. Even so, the content can typically be recycled into other forms of marketing material after publication, such as web content or a flyer.

Which publication an advertorial is intended for dictates its style and content. They can be deployed in newspapers (local and national), magazines (public and trade) and online (article and news sites). The right one to use is the one that your target audience read.

Selecting Computer World magazine for an advertorial about a new pet shop, or placing a piece about an exclusive new fashion range in the village newsletter, isn't going to reap the rewards that, say, an advertorial would in the local newspaper about the burgeoning café culture in the area, featuring your new coffee bar.

The huge range of industry-specific magazines on offer enable you to target some businesses with pinpoint precision.

A manufacturer of parts for farm machinery places an advertorial about the importance of regularly maintaining farm equipment in Farmers Weekly, knowing that the readership coincides almost entirely with their target market.

When you have decided on the ideal publication for your piece, you should ring them up and check that they accept advertorials – and find out how much they charge. They will typically have a price for full page, half page and quarter page pieces. Some publications don't accept advertorials, others stipulate restrictions, many take anything you give them. Before committing yourself, be clear how much space you will require, bearing in mind things like photographs and the size of text used for headlines etc.

Watch out! They may offer to write it for you. Don't be tempted. They will try to sway you with talk of their professionalism and years of experience, but, believe me, journalists, not surprisingly, are quite sneery about advertorials, and won't give it the care and attention it deserves. Also, they don't possess the unrivalled knowledge of your business and your market that you do. They are prone to padding advertorials out with waffle rather than carefully crafting the kind of compelling copy that you can produce (don't worry, you soon will).

❷ WRITING A STORY THAT SELLS

Unfortunately, most of the advertorials you see are little more than promotional fluff. They stand out from the surrounding news stories as if they had 'Naff Commercialism' emblazoned across them in big red letters.

A good advertorial, however, is an enticing piece of journalism. It has genuine substance and displays an understanding of what interests the reader.

There is nothing magical about how this kind of writing is created. Simply follow the advice contained in this section, and your advertorial will be one of the finest examples of influential journalism since Woodward and Bernstein broke the Watergate scandal (well, almost).

Style

If you want the editor to shout things like, 'Stop the press!' and 'Hold the front page!' when you hand in your latest scoop, your writing must be attuned to the house style and in presentational harmony with the rest of the publication.

The following guidelines will help you approach your advertorial with the expertise of a dyed-in-the-wool hack.

℘ Dismiss all ideas of your business from your mind and write as if you are an outsider. That means using the third person at all times – using *he* or *she* instead of *I, they* instead of *we* (as if, instead of writing about your business, you are reporting on someone else's).

℘ Focus only on details that are relevant to the story. For example, resist the urge to come over all hard sell and start writing sentences like, "At these crazy prices you'd be mad to miss them!". Just concentrate on telling the story in a way that will keep the reader engrossed.

O   Before you begin writing, organise your information using the inverted pyramid technique (it's actually a triangle, but pyramid sounds more exotic). The inverted pyramid refers to the way that all the most newsworthy stuff is put into the early section of the article, followed by the less interesting background details, and finally tailing off with the, lets face it, dull but necessary stuff at the end.

Here's a diagram to show how this works:

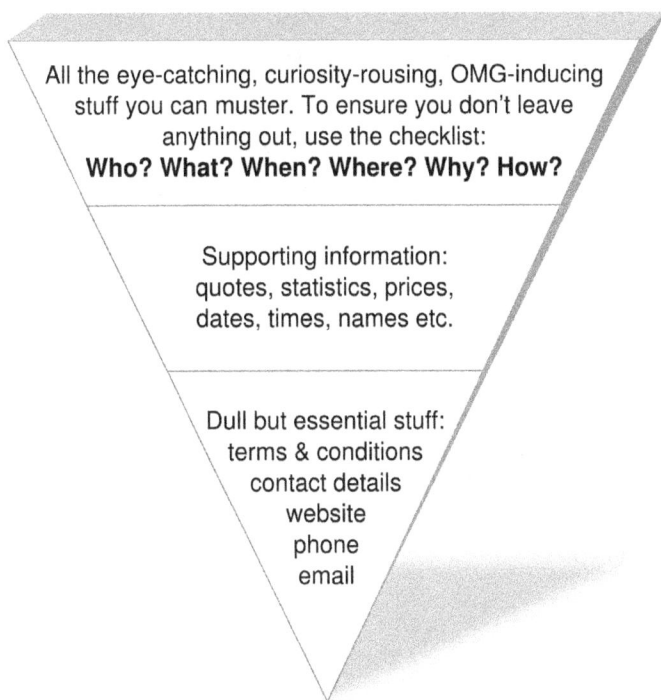

All the eye-catching, curiosity-rousing, OMG-inducing stuff you can muster. To ensure you don't leave anything out, use the checklist:
Who? What? When? Where? Why? How?

Supporting information:
quotes, statistics, prices,
dates, times, names etc.

Dull but essential stuff:
terms & conditions
contact details
website
phone
email

Once you have fully immersed yourself in the persona of a journalist working for the publication you intend to use for your advertorial, and you have collated your information pyramid-style, you are ready to begin writing.

Headline

The headline is your attention grabber. Remember, we are not talking about a commercial headline here, such as those you see in an ad or piece of direct mail, it is a news headline. More specifically, it is a news headline written in the same style as those in the publication in which your advertorial will be placed.

They do vary, just look at the different styles of headlines used for the same story presented in different national newspapers: some are short and to the point, some are longer and more descriptive, some are puns, some are followed by sub-headings, some make you laugh, some make you think the end is nigh... all for a story about a well-known footballer with an ankle injury.

So, you need a headline that:

- Is newsy, not salesy
- Fits with the house style
- Will knock readers' socks off

Plucking such a gem as this out of thin air is difficult. You can juggle words around all day and get nowhere. However, you can shortcut the process dramatically.

As mentioned before, there are two fundamental themes for an advertorial, and each has a formula that will reveal a suitable headline:

How to create a headline for *a problem facing the readers (that your business can help solve)*:

1. Complete the sentence: 'Solve {the problem}'

2. Fine-tune as necessary

How to create a headline for an event (involving your business) that will interest readers:

1. Complete the sentence: '{The most special thing} at {the event}'

2. Fine-tune as necessary

In both cases, you are offering the reader something they will want, whether it is a solution to a problem or information they will be interested in. Do this, and a headline will emerge that will have socks flying off all over the place.

> Lumisecure Security Lighting is a small business selling and fitting outdoor security lighting. It is autumn and the nights are getting darker, the perfect time to plant a piece in the local newspaper about shadowy premises and the shadowy characters they can attract – unless, of course, you have suitable security lighting.

A bad headline would be:

Lumisecure Security Lighting

This would only attract avid followers of Lumisecure Security Lighting.

What about:

Dazzling Prices on Security Lighting!!!

This may have more pizzazz, but it will only be read by people actively looking for security lighting, making it no better than a cheap advertisement.

The theme of the advertorial – dark nights – is the problem. So, using the 'Solve {the problem}' technique, we arrive at:

Solve Dark Nights

Fine tune this into a more meaningful kind of language, and you arrive at:

Don't Be Afraid of the Dark

If the publication was not a local newspaper, but a trade journal for janitors working in schools and colleges, for example, the resulting headline would be different. Here, the problem would be the security of a large building and the students within it. The reader would be actively looking for practical guidance, which allows a more direct style of problem-solving language to be used:

Lighting and Security for Winter

Subhead

Headlines such as these could, if the publication's house style allows, be bolstered by a subhead that hints at the solution you are about to describe. For example:

> ## Don't Be Afraid of the Dark
>
> **Bright ideas to make your home
> a safer place this winter**

And:

> ## Lighting and Security for Winter
>
> **Prevent break-ins and keep students safe**

Byline

If the 'proper' stories in the paper have a line under the headline saying something like...

> **Special report by Jilly Gibson**

...then you do one as well. It will add realism and credibility to your piece.

Opener

The first paragraph of your advertorial is the place to convince the reader that this is something that they really must take serious notice of. It must raise an issue that is of interest to the reader and indicate that you are about to divulge the solution or information they have been longing to hear. Let them know straight away what is in it for them;

a problem solved, an easier life, happiness! Whatever it is, tell them now.

Lumisecure Security Lighting begin their advertorial with:

> The clocks have gone back and, as the nights draw in, we are all more aware of home security. But what can be done to ensure your property isn't a target for opportunistic thieves? Fortunately, there are a number of simple lighting solutions to brighten your home and make thieves think twice.

Body

Now you are into the meat of the story, your objective is to first, explain the issue and second, introduce your company.

1 Explain the issue

Address the problem or event you have identified by referring to the kind of products and services you provide. To avoid bombarding the reader with a full-on sales pitch, mix in some wisdom with your solution. Sharing your expertise here will help to put your products and services into context when you drop them into the narrative.

An interior designer suggests ways to make the most of small rooms, giving examples from their range of solutions.

A property maintenance company gives advice on how to prepare homes for winter, while subtly referring to the services they provide.

2 Introduce your company

Focus on what makes you a leader in this particular niche, what makes you special. Don't bore readers with every detail of your business, from where the boss went to school to the amusing story of how you acquired the office cat, and don't just cut and paste your About Us web page. No one's interested.

By tackling both of these objectives, you will be dealing with all the items on the top (i.e. bottom) of your inverted pyramid. Whatever you do, don't pad things out just to fill up space. Readers respond better to fresh, concise writing, so keep it to the point. In fact, go out of your way to break things up with bullet points and subheads, if the house style permits, and include plenty of supporting information, such as...

- Facts and figures, including graphs, tables, timelines, charts etc. where applicable

- Quotations from real people and real experts

- Images that add to the story with meaningful captions (see Visuals)

This will provide the reader with respite from an otherwise unrelenting barrage of words and add integrity and interest to your piece.

Lumisecure continue their advertorial with:

A recent study found that a shocking 93% of houses that were burgled during the winter months had no external lighting. This figure clearly demonstrates the deterrent effect of outdoor security lighting. So why don't more of us have it?

David Palmer, Chief Crime Prevention Officer for North Devon, says, "This is a serious concern, yet it is very frustrating as it is so easy to resolve. Basic lighting outside the home is enough to deter most burglars. When they see that, 9 times out of 10 they move on."

So why are so many people not taking the simple step of having security lights fitted? According to local supplier, Lumisecure Security Lighting, located on Barnstaple retail park, the problem is that there is too much choice. As Jim Scott, owner of Lumisecure explained, "There has never been so much external lighting to choose from as there is now, and it has never been so affordable, but people are confused by the sheer choice on offer."

After a brief look around the Lumisecure store, it is clear what he means. There is everything here from large external floodlights to solar powered garden lights to ingeniously concealed security lights and much more besides. However, help is at hand.

In an attempt to maximise the number of homes in the area that are safely lit this winter, Lumisecure are offering free home-visits in the run up to Christmas to advise people on the type of lighting that would be best for them.

Visuals

A well chosen picture can communicate even a complex point in an instant. So don't waste valuable space with a photograph of the Managing Director standing outside their premises grinning at the camera, or a picture of an employee sat behind a desk pretending to be on the telephone. Captivating though these images might seem to the business's employees, they have no appeal to the customers that constitute your readers. Use images to bring to life the issue at the heart of the article, and use captions to add meaning to what is shown in the image.

> Lumisecure incorporate a photograph of a well-lit house next to an unlit house on a dark street with the caption: 'If you were a thief, which house would you burgle?'.

On a practical matter, you should check with the publication if there are any stipulations for the kind of images you are supplying. As well as format (.jpg, .png etc), they might restrict its size in terms of pixels or megabytes. When creating your own images, set the resolution as high as possible. A low resolution snap may look great on a mobile phone, but it will look blurred and amateurish on the page of a glossy magazine.

Ending

What you don't want to happen is for your potential customer to finish the article thinking, 'How very interesting' then turn the page and start browsing the next item designed to catch their attention.

The final paragraph must tell the reader what to do. Here you can allow yourself to step slightly away from editorial territory towards ad land and deliver a powerful call to action along with contact details and whatever it takes to make it as easy as possible for the reader to call your office / place an order / visit your website / sign up... or whatever it is that you want them to do.

Lumisecure conclude their advertorial with:

The fear of a house break-in will become a sad reality for many local people this winter. Yet taking steps to prevent it couldn't be easier. For free advice about security lighting or to arrange a free home visit, call Lumisecure on 01254 32263 or visit their website at www.lumisecure.co.uk

Here is the full Lumisecure advertorial:

Don't be afraid of the dark

Bright ideas to make your home a safer place this winter

Special report by Felicity Dunn

The clocks have gone back and, as the nights draw in, we are all more aware of home security. But what can be done to ensure your property isn't a target for opportunistic thieves? Fortunately, there are a number of simple lighting solutions to brighten your home and make thieves think twice.

A recent study found that a shocking 93% of houses that were burgled during the winter months had no external lighting. This figure clearly demonstrates the deterrent effect of outdoor security lighting. So why don't more of us have it?

If you were a thief, which house would you burgle?

David Palmer, Chief Crime Prevention Officer for North Devon, says, "This is a serious concern, yet it is very frustrating as it is so easy to resolve. Basic lighting outside the home is enough to deter most burglars. When they see that, 9 times out of 10 they move on."

So why are so many people not taking the simple step of having security lights fitted? According to local supplier, Lumisecure Security Lighting, located on Barnstaple retail park, the problem is that there is too much choice. As Jim Scott, owner of Lumisecure explained, "There has never been so much external lighting to choose from as there is now, and it has never been so affordable, but people are confused by the sheer choice on offer."

After a brief look around the Lumisecure store, it is clear what he means. There is everything here from large external floodlights to solar powered garden lights to ingeniously concealed security lights and much more besides. However, help is at hand.

In an attempt to maximise the number of homes in the area that are safely lit this winter, Lumisecure are offering free home-visits in the run up to Christmas to advise people on the type of lighting that would be best for them.

The fear of a house break-in will become a sad reality for many local people this winter. Yet taking steps to prevent it couldn't be easier.

For free advice about security lighting or to arrange a free home visit, call Lumisecure on 01254 32263 or visit their website at www.lumisecure.co.uk

BLOGS

Build a brand, boost business and
blog with bang!

I f a website is a business's shop window, the blog is an audacious child that has sneaked into the display to have some fun.

Successful business blogs are unrefined, unpredictable and unmissable. They give readers a regular reason to visit a site, and they provide businesses with the means to build a personal relationship with their customers.

WHAT'S IN THIS CHAPTER?

❶ STRATEGY

Writing a blog is easy – but writing one that reaps all the marketing rewards that business blogging can bring requires some strategic thinking before you even set a finger on your computer keyboard.

A winning strategy puts the nuts and bolts of the author's publicity machine firmly in place (of course, the apparent author will most likely be your client). Only then can you set off into the blogosphere with a clear destination in mind and a precise understanding of how you will get there.

Objectives

The objective of a business blog is not the same as the objective of most other forms of marketing.

> *What your blog is aiming to achieve*
> A blog is not about getting your message out, it is about drawing prospective customers in.

Using a blog as a podium from which to advertise products and services would be entirely unfruitful as no one would want to read it. Writing interesting posts that appeal to your business's target market, however, will bring prospective customers to your door.

As well as this universal objective, your blog needs to have a more specific goal. Look at the following list and see which one most applies to your blogging intentions:

- Move the website up the search engine rankings
- Draw more people into the website
- Position the business as an authority in its field
- Build awareness of the brand
- Gain understanding of potential customers
- Develop a rapid response facility that enables you to get the word out quickly
- Cross-promote to other online activities, such as social media sites
- Analyse comments on each blog, like an instant focus group

Concentrating all your blogging efforts on one of these goals will, in fact, increase your chances of accomplishing all of them.

A manufacturer of 'green' products focuses on building their brand's credentials by blogging about all things environmentally-friendly. This sends out the right brand message and gives people a reason to visit, which leads to numerous other business benefits.

Over time, a customer-friendly blog with a clear objective will become a focal point for precisely the kind of people that some companies spend fortunes trying to reach via traditional advertising. When a successful blog begins to generate a buzz in an online community, it can turn the website into a hub for that particular kind of news and information.

Technical stuff

» Hosting – Where the blog lives online

Your blog has to be hosted – which basically means it needs a home on the internet. This can either be on one of the free blogging websites, such as WordPress or Blogger (just Google 'blogging websites' to learn more) where it will have its own address (www.yourblog.blogsite.com), or it can have its own page on your existing website (www.yourwebsite.com/blog).

The former has all the self-contained convenience of a rented bedsit. Perfect, therefore, for someone simply wishing to post their personal musings. The latter is like having a room in your own home, where you can run around in the nude, paint the walls any colour you like and keep chickens under the bed (metaphorically speaking). If your business already has a website in place (and if they don't, they should), this is the best option.

The company that hosts the website will be able to advise on any additional cost, if any, involved in hosting a blog.

» Platform – How the blog is created and maintained

The software that you use to generate your blog is your platform. The most commonly used platforms are WordPress, TypePad, Blog.com and Blogger (just Google 'blogging platform' to learn more). They are typically free, easy to use and include useful extras. Ask the company that hosts the website if they have a particular recommendation.

Time (how not to waste it writing blogs)

Unlike a one-off advertorial or piece of direct mail, a blog is an on-going and potentially time-consuming process. To someone with other things to do this may seem like too much of a commitment. Thankfully, it doesn't have to be that hard. Once you get into the swing of things, writing a blog post can take up as little time as (and coincide with) a coffee break.

⏱ Look out for the QUICKTIPs throughout this chapter. These nuggets of inside knowledge are designed to prevent your blog taking over your life, making the process swift, effortless and enjoyable.

Length

People don't visit business blogs to read a lengthy essay. Keep your posts short, fresh and to the point. Around 300 to 400 words is ample to make an impact. This wordcount is not set in stone, so use it as a guide rather than an objective in itself. 200 worthwhile words will generate a better outcome than 600 worthless ones. A post that grows as it covers an increasing range of issues can be split into two or more separate posts.

⏱ Keep it simple: One issue per post.

Frequency

Posting once a week at a regular time is fine. As long as you are giving your readers something fresh, they'll keep coming back. Whatever your posting frequency, try to stick to it. If your readers don't know whether there will be anything new there or not, they won't bother looking.

Put some blog posts away for a rainy day. Write three or four non-topical pieces before you even post your first piece. Then, you can put these to use whenever you are too busy/ill/chilled-out-on-holiday to write a fresh one.

⏱ Regular is more important than often.

❷ WHAT TO WRITE ABOUT

A blog that is little more than an empty collection of words with nothing to offer the reader is like a wannabe celebrity who finally finds themselves in front of the cameras and has absolutely nothing to say. They just stand there grinning while the viewer loses interest.

Your blog needs to have substance so that, when it is in the public eye, it can seize the opportunity for all it's worth.

Find your niche

Writing within your business's area of interest will draw people towards your website who also have an interest in what your business does. Identifying your specific niche is a little trickier, however, than simply stating what it is your business does.

Before you think about what to write, you need to take a moment to think about what you are not writing.

» Your blog is not a newsletter

Newsletters are too corporate. There should be some distance between your blog and your business. Imagine sitting in that nice café down the road where you can relax away from your work and have a good chat with your readers – that is the kind of detachment we are after.

» Your blog is not a sales piece

When people read blogs they do not want to encounter some barefaced sales spiel. When faced with this kind of ad-blog, readers, quite understandably, recoil from the site, never to return again. Readers won't mind you referencing particular products, but if it becomes the whole raison d'être of the piece.

» Your blog is not an online journal

You are blogging with the ultimate aim of promoting your business, not catching the eye of a publisher. So write about your subject with passion and personality, but not with a deliberate on-going narrative.

To summarise... your blog should promote your products and services without being a blatant sales pitch, and it should beguile the reader without straying into story-telling. To turn this into something more tangible, you also need to consider the people you are writing the blog for. So ask yourself: What do potential customers want to read about?

In addressing your customers' concerns, you may refer to your products and services, you may share a relevant anecdote, but you will primarily be taking your lead from what they want to read about. Tap into this pool of subject matter and your desired readership will warm to your blog, and your business.

The prospective customers of a business offering gardening products and services to local residents do not want to read about the business per se, but they do want to read about local, garden-related goings on.

After letting it be known in all the right places that their blog offers news and expert insight into such things as the wonderful display of colour at the local park, the blog will attract precisely the kind of people that will be interested in the products and services that are available on the company's website.

Gardenews

Have you seen the colours at the town park this year? Considering the time of year, it's remarkable, and the council have done a super job as ever in keeping the weeds at bay.

Here's a run-down of what you can see, and how you can create a similar display in your own garden...

If you're a keen gardener, a grow your own enthusiast, or a beginner in the world of gardening, you'll find regular news, tips and advice right here.

21579 visitors

Providing local news and views in this way would not work for, say, a small engineering plant looking to sell internationally. Their prospective customers may want to read about much more industry-related topics. Responding to your target audiences' particular interests is crucial.

And when you have identified your niche, stick to it.

If the same gardening business suddenly started blogging about interpretive dance, it would undo any kudos they had previously cultivated.

Specific topics

There is an endless assortment of topics to write a blog about. You have already narrowed the field down considerably by identifying your particular niche. Now you face the task of selecting something specific to write about whenever it is time to post your latest dispatch.

There is one thing you should always remember when deciding what to write about.

The BIG rule of blog topics
Treat each post as a single comment on an issue, not an all-embracing analysis.

Choosing a wide-ranging subject will result in a superficial overview, using up lots of potential topics in a single post. Save that kind of analysis for a fully-fledged report.

A clothes designer wants to write about workplace fashion. That subject is so broad it could fill a library. So, they focus on one small item for each post, such as telling readers about what they saw someone wearing on the 08:15 train from Alexandra Park Station this morning.

🕐 Readers can find broad overviews anywhere, but your unique insight is something worth seeking out.

30 starting points

Out of an immeasurably vast quantity of possible topics to blog about, here are 30 starting points that should trigger a stream of suitable subjects. Not all of them will be appropriate for your niche, but they will help you to get thinking about the kind of things that will interest prospective readers/customers.

1   Answer a question that customers often ask

2   Set straight a common misconception

3   Skim social networking to see if there is anything 'trending' about the industry

4   React to news stories relating to your business's products, services or industry

5   Turn a customer testimonial into a post

6   Describe how the business is participating in an event

7   Highlight the weaknesses of your competitors (subtly)

8   Describe something special about the way you make your products or deal with customers

9   Request feedback on new ideas your business is proposing

10   Describe how your products or services have saved the day at one time

11   Give a sneak preview of something your business is planning to do in the near future

12   Give a how-to lesson

13   Do a list of '10 thing you didn't know about...'

14   Quote an inspiring speaker related to your sector

15   Tell readers about what you saw at a trade show

16   Explain how your product or service solves a problem

17   Describe a day-in-the-life at your company

18   Use a celebrity name ('Which of our home made jams would George Clooney choose?')

19 Talk about errors you have made, and how you resolved them

20 Innovative applications of your products or services

21 Look beyond your business – do your suppliers have any news you could relate?

22 Adapt case studies into a more personal style

23 Profile a big shot from your industry (or a little shot that makes a big impact)

24 Explain changes to your products or services

25 The story behind your products and services (e.g. where your raw materials come from)

26 Expand on answers to your FAQs

27 Review a (relevant) book, product or service (not your own)

28 Profile a member of staff

29 Compare the old way of doing your business with the new

30 Look at other business's blogs for inspiration.

⏱ Choose something simple and obvious to write about rather than struggling each time to come up with the ultimate topic.

❸ HOW TO WRITE IT

To someone not accustomed to writing a regular, lengthy narrative for a specific audience, becoming a blogger can be a daunting experience, causing normal linguistic aptitude to wilt under the pressure.

Fortunately, the creation of each post can be turned into an almost mechanical process. Once you become familiar with how it is done, you'll be posting blogs as easily as chickens lay eggs.

Find your style

As Frank Sinatra summed it up so tunefully in the film 'Robin and the 7 Hoods', You've either got or you haven't got style. With some people, it just comes effortlessly. With others, it needs a little work.

An engaging writing style is a pre-requisite of blogging. Without it, you risk disappearing into the blandness of web wallpaper – there, but easily ignored. Thankfully, this elusive stand-out-from-the-crowd quality isn't just the result of a God-given gift bestowed on only the lucky few. Style is like a voice: we all have our own, but sometimes outside help is needed before we feel comfortable sharing it with the rest of the world.

Here are some tips to help you liberate your blogging voice:

» Suit yourself

Your style must fit your own character. It could be humorous, academic, conversational, informative, cheeky... whatever, as long as it suits you, your business and your subject.

» Be informal (but not too informal)

While blogging is a more laid-back kind of writing than the rest of a website, it should not be slapdash. Dispense with corporate prose, but still aim for quality writing.

» Be natural

Don't make it unnecessarily difficult by struggling to put on an act, using obscure words to sound intellectual, for example. It's too time consuming, it's hard work, it's not fun and it doesn't work. Stick with words that come naturally to you.

» Keep it simple

Pitch your language at the people you intend reading your blog. This usually means, no jargon. Jargon may be a part of daily conversation within the business, but it will only irritate anyone on the outside. If jargon is unavoidable, include a clear definition.

» Be upfront

Address your reader directly, as if it is just one person you are talking to (initially, it probably is). This allows you to communicate in a candid, face-to-face manner.

» Keep it short

Short sentences are easier to write and nicer to read than long ones.

⏱ The easiest and the best writing style is always your own.

Create an outline

Okay. You know your objective, you have found your niche, you have decided upon your subject and you have uncovered your personal style. Now you just need to write something.

Rather than facing the prospect of staring for hours at an empty screen wondering how to tackle the first sentence, sketch out the gist of what you want to say in outline form.

The outline simply covers:

1 What the post is about

2 The steps involved in spelling this out to the reader

You could think about your blog post as a story, because people enjoy reading stories much more than adverts or lists of facts. A story draws the reader in and gives them something to follow. An outline for a story might be:

   O   The background and reasons for the story

   O   The problems that the characters in the story faced

   O   How you thought about those problems

   O   How you solved the problems

   O   The happy ending

A wedding photographer wanting to post a blog about a great group shot taken at a recent wedding might begin with the following outline:

- How I took a great group shot that wasn't the usual boring kind of thing

- Describe the problems usually faced: People looking too formal and fed up with photographer bossing them around

- Describe the wedding I photographed last weekend: Struggling to get a nice group shot / three botched attempts / people getting cross with me

- Then, gathered them together for a final attempt / took picture and shouted 'Got it!' / everyone relaxed / then I really took the picture – capturing everyone looking happy and natural

Simple, huh? But it is a good way to get started. Without a basic structure like this, blogs tend to ramble on and leave the reader feeling bored and bewildered. An outline helps to keep things reined in.

⏱ A simple, but complete, outline is better than an elaborate, but incomplete one.

Flesh it out

Once you have sketched out your outline, expand a little on each element. Don't worry about grammar and spelling for now, just get the key details written down.

The wedding photographer fleshes out his outline like this:

- Great informal group shot
- Group shots are hardest because there are more people – all of whom have to look good I've dealt with many challenging moments over the years (such as.?)
- But last weekend, I thought I had met my match. At the end of a long day, I set about capturing the 'big one', the group shot of everyone that was present.
- After a series of struggles getting them all into position, I had three attempts at taking the picture.
- And I wasn't happy with any of them – I like to have some life in my pictures. However, the crowd were getting restless and I knew I only had one more chance at success.
- I primed the group for one last attempt. I looked through the viewfinder then shouted, 'Got it!', in a triumphant voice.
- The mood immediately changed. Everyone relaxed and smiled as the strain was lifted.
- And then I really took the picture. Here it is. (show pic)

🕐 Use plain facts and language – but if any good words or phrases come into your head, jot them down.

Add vital content

There are a number of essential ingredients that will beef up your blog and give it its all-important marketing edge. Include the following in every post:

» Keywords

New customers won't be able to find you if the search engines can't find you first. For them to know you exist you need to use keywords. Keywords are the words and phrases your intended readership will use when searching for something relevant to your blog's subject matter. Your keywords are used in a number of locations.

Keywords in the text

Put the most important keywords in your headline. Then, drop them in throughout the text, especially within the first 200 characters, which carries more weight with search engines. This should not be done at the expense of quality and meaning, as the natural way you write can include relevant keywords without even trying.

⏱ Write your keywords at the top of the document before you begin. This will keep them in your mind and help you include them naturally in the text.

Keywords in the image alternate text

As with any image on the internet, when you insert one in your blog, you can provide 'alternate text' that will appear if a visitor cannot load the image for whatever reason. This text is also a sneaky place to include some unseen keywords.

⏱ No one (hardly ever) sees alternate text, so don't worry about creating meaningful sentences, just chuck the keywords in.

Keywords in the source code

Source code is the computer programming that makes your web page what it is. Within it are the page's Title and Description. These tell search engines what your page is all about, so they should contain your most important keywords. If you are using WordPress as your platform you can use the 'All in one SEO Pack' to specify these fields. Alternatively, you could speak to the web hosting company who may be able to help you with it. (See further discussion of Source Code in the Websites chapter of this book.)

Keywords in the URL

The URL is the web address of the page where your blog post resides. Google et al take great heed of the URL, so incorporating your main keywords there can have a big impact on search engine rankings.

For example, rather than calling your page 'blog #27' or whatever, give it a more meaningful title such as, 'Indian Head Massage', so the web page would be called something like:

```
www.yourwebsite.com/indian-head-massage
```

⏱ A small number of well-placed keywords is better than too many, which can make your blog post appear badly written.

» Headline

The headline of each blog post should use your keywords, be descriptive and be enticing.

Put all this into a succinct headline and you have something that your prospective readership will take notice of.

The wedding photographer's headline is designed to:

> ➤ Use the most powerful keywords: 'wedding' and 'photography'

> ➤ Be descriptive: It's about a technique used to take a great group photo

> ➤ Be enticing: Implying that the text will reveal some sort of secret is always inviting.

So a fitting headline for this blog is:

A PHOTOGRAPHY TRICK
FOR A WEDDING PIC

🕐 It is often easier to write the blog first then decide on the headline last.

» Sub-headings

Dividing the text into manageable chunks using relevant sub headings and bullet points where applicable can add emphasis and make it more appealing to someone giving it a preliminary scan.

» Bullet points

Unwieldy, overly long paragraphs can often be made more reader-friendly by employing bullet points to break things up.

» Photos and video

Your blog does not have to simply be a written composition. Because it is on the internet, it can incorporate all sorts of other media. Well-chosen visuals can bring your words to life. Just ensure they are relevant to what you are writing about.

» Links

Including links that lead readers away from your blog may seem counter-intuitive, but the benefits of links far outweigh any danger of readers disappearing along them. There are three types of links, each with their own advantage:

- Links to external sites that relate to what you are discussing will give your post more substance and credibility.

- Links to pages within your own website will draw readers in, where they will discover what products and services are there for them.

- Links to your older posts will give them a new lease of life.

⏱ After you have written the blog, look over it for any words or phrases that would make suitable links.

» A call to action

Unless you just want readers to read your blog, and nothing more, you need to tell them what to do next.

This may be to:

- Visit a specific page on the website
- Ring up to place an order
- Sign up for a newsletter
- Follow a link to a related post
- Read an advert for a forthcoming event
- Leave a comment

» Social networking buttons

You can dramatically broaden the reach of your blog by making it easy to share via social networking. This can be achieved by listing a selection of social networking buttons at the end of your post: LinkedIn, Facebook, Twitter, StumbleUpon, Digg, Reddit... and don't forget good old-fashioned email.

Your chosen blog software will have a way to automate this for you. Readers simply click on their preferred button or buttons to share your blog with their wider network.

If your post then strikes a chord with this second wave of readers and they decide to share it with their network, your blog (including all the links and other promotional content) will spread through your target clientèle like the plague (but in a nice way).

The wedding photographer's blog post uses the following vital content:

Keywords: wedding, photography, photographer, Surrey, bride, groom, Guildford, Dorking

URL: www.johnstewartphotography.com/blog/wedding-photographer-trick

Source Code Title: Surrey Wedding Photographer | Ashford Wedding Photography | Wedding Photographer Guildford, Dorking | John Stewart Photography

Source Code Description: John Stewart Photography. Stylish and contemporary Wedding Photographer in Ashford, Surrey providing outstanding natural wedding photography

Here is the photographer's completed blog post.

Photo Tips
with John

A PHOTOGRAPHY TRICK FOR A WEDDING PIC

Group shots at weddings are the hardest pictures of all for two reasons.

First, it is usually the last one to be done, meaning that everyone is fed up of being photographed by then. Second, with more people involved, there are more things to go wrong.

Throughout my years as a wedding photographer, I have had to deal with many challenging issues while trying to capture the perfect group shot...

- a bride with a sneezing fit

- feuding family members who won't stand together

- a missing guest (later found in the loo)

...but, as you can see from my portfolio, all have worked out well in the end.

Last weekend, however, I thought I had met my match. It was a local wedding in Guildford, Surrey, and photographing the bride and groom had been a joy and had worked out wonderfully (you can see some of their photographs here). The end of a particularly long day was drawing near, so I set about capturing the 'big one', the group shot of everyone present at the wedding.

After a series of struggles (similar to the ones that I discussed in a previous blog) bringing all 86 wedding-goers into position, I took the picture. Two attempts later and I wasn't happy with any of them. The group in the picture didn't look like the people I had seen moments earlier, laughing and joking with each other. They looked stiff, formal and, to be frank, dull.

And, the crowd were getting restless

This bugged me because I like to show some real life in all my wedding pictures, even the more formal ones, such as the notoriously difficult group photograph. However, the crowd were getting restless and were in no mood for indulging my artistic sensibilities. I could already see a couple of aged aunties eyeing their glasses of sherry back in the snug and I knew I only had one more chance at success.

So, in this increasingly antagonistic atmosphere, I primed the group for one final attempt. I looked through the viewfinder then shouted, 'Got it!', in a loud, triumphant voice.

The mood immediately changed. Everyone relaxed and laughed as the strain was lifted from their shoulders. Even the two aged aunts clapped their hands in joy and gave each other a beaming smile at the prospect of getting back to their sherry.

And then I really took the picture. Here it is.

I love my job. Especially when I am capturing magical moments like these. Let me know what you think of the picture in the comments below.

And, if you are looking for a wedding photographer in Surrey or beyond that knows all the tricks of the trade – click here to get in touch.

❹ WHEN BLOGS TURN BAD

After the blog has been up and running for a while, there will most likely come a time when you think to yourself: 'Wait a minute! This blog is taking up too much of my time and too many of my brain cells. This epiphany will typically strike at a moment when you feel the blog is becoming less a fun piece of marketing communications and more the bane of your life.

Like a cute puppy that seemed such a good idea at the time, a blog can soon turn into a high-maintenance monster. Here's how to show it who's boss (that would be you, by the way).

My brain hurts!

If you find yourself struggling to think of something to write about each time you have a blog post to dispatch, something is wrong. It shouldn't be that hard. In fact, it should be easy. So, if you are repeatedly finding that your ideas cupboard is bare, and you feel like ripping the door off its hinges, there are four possible responses:

1   Carry on regardless. This is a bad idea. Writing a business blog is not an endurance test, it is supposed to be fun, liberating, therapeutic. Life's too short to struggle through self-induced challenges.

2   Give up. Despite all the effort I have put into writing this chapter of the book, I think that quitting the blog would be fair enough if the time and effort you are putting into it is not reflected in the marketing results you are getting out of it. Maybe your energy would be better spent on other marketing activities or a different type of blog. But before you do, please

read to the end of this section, just in case there is a solution at hand.

3   Get someone else to do it. You could delegate the responsibility to a colleague who may be better suited to the task. This could be someone with specialist insight, for example. They could flesh out the outline, and you could take it from there. As long as the new blogger sticks to the hard and fast rules for maximising marketing returns that I have outlined, this should not be a problem. You could even recruit a team of blog-starters.

4   Think small. Remember the BIG rule I mentioned earlier (so big it merits capital letters): Treat each post as a single comment on an issue, not an all-embracing analysis. Well here is a BIG analogy to make it even clearer: Don't spend time searching for a forest when all you require is a twig. The world, not least the world wide web, is bursting with great ideas to blog about. If you are struggling to find a subject, you are looking for something too momentous. Take a step back and notice the small details. You'll be surprised how a minor point can grow into an interesting blog post once you start tapping away at the keyboard about it. This single point, for example, has now reached 129 words!

Everyone's a critic!

There is an option of whether or not to allow comments on your blog. The comments people leave in response to what you have written can provide valuable feedback that is highly useful for business decision-making. It can also allow the business to present a personal face that shows they are there listening to customers and happy to help.

On the other hand, it can open the door to some less welcome comments. Some can even be quite hurtful. However, there are ways of dealing with them that can work to your advantage.

- *℗* Remember that everyone can read your response, so keep it polite and respectful, and you will come across as such, whatever the original comment was about.

- *℗* If someone expresses a complaint, be sure to be seen to tackle it head on and promptly.

- *℗* Sometimes a dismissive comment can be a golden opportunity to expand on the issue concerned and introduce additional facts, figures and other information.

- *℗* Be willing to learn from others' comments, however disagreeably put. Simply replying with, 'An interesting point. Thanks, I'll bear it in mind.' is often the best response.

- *℗* If someone says you have made a mistake, and you have, don't try and hide from the fact. Admit it, apologise and modify your post.

Comments can be immensely useful things, but if you do allow them on your blog, you should moderate them to make sure that they don't include anything uncalled-for, such as spam, impoliteness or self-serving links.

If you do find yourself on the receiving end of any negative comments, whatever you do, don't take them personally. You can't please all of the people all of the time, but some people have nothing better to do than write stupid comments on blogs.

Where are the readers?!

There are few things more disheartening than to write a real bobby-dazzler of a blog and for it to go unnoticed by those that would most appreciate it. To gain maximum marketing advantage from your blog, you need to be drawing in large elements of your target market. If this is not happening, try these tips. In fact, try them anyway – the more high-value readers of your blog you have the better.

- *O* Check that you are implementing all the techniques I mentioned way back in the 'Add vital content' section.

- *O* Check that your keywords are worthwhile ones. You may be tailoring your blog to the wrong audience. Try typing different words and phrases into Google to see what brings up relevant results.

- *O* Use the homepage of your main business website to promote your blog. You could simply have a button linking to the blog or you could have a panel showing the first few lines of the latest posts and an offer to 'read more…'.

- *O* Refer to your blog on social media. For example, provide links on the company's Facebook page and tweet about the latest post. If your business does not have a social media presence yet, check out the relevant chapters in this book.

BROCHURES

Write a corporate brochure that people actually want to read

C orporate brochures sell a business, rather than specific products (its more brazen sibling, the sales brochure, is dealt with in the Product Descriptions chapter of this book).

Here, you will discover how to create that rarest of creatures: a corporate brochure that does much more than sit on the coffee table in reception acting as a coaster.

WHAT'S IN THIS CHAPTER?

❶ THE TRUTH ABOUT CORPORATE BROCHURES

Corporate brochures may be loved by the people who write them, but they are loathed by everyone else. No one in their right mind would pick one up and read it for their own enjoyment.

Unless you write a good one, that is. And to do that you must first understand what they are capable of and why many of them fail.

Corporate brochures are old fashioned

Quaint, frail and somewhat outdated, the corporate brochure seems like an elderly ancestor of the more youthful and dynamic website. And yes, most modern brochures are little more than a printed and bound version of the company website. The only difference being that, by the time they are printed and distributed, they are usually obsolete. So isn't it time we packed this analogue has-been off to the great pulping plant in the sky?

Well, though it may share the same genetic make up as its digital descendant, a corporate brochure does possess a number of unrivalled attributes:

» Physicality

A brochure gives prospective customers something they can hang onto. Something they can carry, slip inside a briefcase or sit on their desk. Something they can read wherever and whenever suits them. Something that can be left with a prospective client after a meeting or sent to a potential customer in lieu of a visit.

» Credibility

Anyone can have a website, but only a reputable business would put in the effort to produce a brochure. Or so people believe. A well-crafted corporate brochure reassures potential customers and potential investors alike that you are not just some 'here today, gone tomorrow' outfit.

» Immediacy

Like a flyer or a TV advert, a brochure doesn't wait for people to stumble across it. It gets straight in front of the intended target's eyes, giving them something to deal with now.

» Influence

A brochure is a slick package that can form part of a press pack to hand out to journalists, or a submission to anyone else that may have an impact on your business, such as politicians and other decision makers.

» Versatility

Like a teenager that is forced to admit that their parents are not actually as uncool as they previously thought, a company website can incorporate an online version of the brochure for visitors to view and download.

If a business takes advantage of these unique features, the corporate brochure starts to look less like an old has-been and more like a valuable weapon in their marketing armoury – one that should be wielded at every opportunity.

Corporate brochures are boring

There, I've said it.

Well, a vast majority of them are. I know they are every company's pride and joy, proudly put on show whenever there is a client to impress, but it has to be said: they are dull.

They bang on about themselves, filling pages with tiresome clichés, lifeless company histories and dreary images. They read like one long ego trip designed to anaesthetise the unfortunate reader. They feebly try to sell, rather than inform. They are badly written and they lack any kind of narrative or direction.

The trouble is, corporate brochures are like bad breath: no one will ever tell you that yours stinks. Instead, people pretend to be interested by perusing its pages, while secretly reeling from the uninspiring, self-indulgent blandness that they are having to endure.

Well, I've had enough of businesses parading their dreadful brochures like they contained a secret treasure map or a long lost Shakespeare sonnet. It is time to create a corporate brochure that people will actually enjoy reading and will actually achieve something worthwhile.

❷ PLAN

You can create effective business brochures without an expensive photographer or graphic designer. But try to get by without a clear idea of who the target readership is, what they want and how you are going to give it to them, and your brochure could do more harm than good.

As American baseball legend Yogi Berra famously said: "If you don't know where you are going, you'll end up someplace else." I don't think he was talking about corporate brochures, but the same approach applies.

Who's in charge?

Everyone in the business should work on the brochure, right? No! Creating content along the principles of a hippy commune, where everyone has equal say over what goes in, will give it all the appeal of a communal kaftan.

As it gets passed around for each person to add their bit, then passed around again for everyone to comment on (which they will, because everyone feels they have to change something in order to look like they know what they are talking about) – all impact, clarity and consistency will be lost as the brochure gradually mutates into the version least disliked by everyone.

The 'design by committee' approach never works. What is needed is a dictatorship (but without the uniforms and all the shouting). One person to take control of the project. Someone that can put themselves in the mind of the intended reader. This would typically be the business's marketing manager, or if there isn't anyone capable of fulfilling the role, it's probably you.

Before writing, interview the contributors
Ask specific questions that readers will want
answering. Maybe draw up a questionnaire that
covers all the information each part of the
business needs to provide.

Who are you writing for?

The uppermost thing in your mind when you write your
corporate brochure should be the prospective reader.
Everything in there is for them and them alone. Every piece
of information that is included must be there because it
benefits them, and expressed in a way that resonates with
their needs.

The reader is your leader:

1   Who are they?

2   Why are they be interested in the business?

3   What are their specific needs?

4   How can you satisfy their specific needs?

5   What action do they need to take?

These five questions provide the raison d'etre of the
brochure. If you begin bashing away at your keyboard
before you have precise and detailed answers to these
questions, your carefully crafted content will have all the
impact of a bouquet of flowers delivered to the wrong
address.

What's the story?

A brochure with a meaningful progression provides readers with a sequence of events that unfold to reveal a clear vision of what a business can do for them. It gives a logical flow to otherwise formless content and can turn a piece of business writing into a Dan Brown-esque page-turner.

Fail to collate your information into any kind of narrative structure, and your brochure will be as directionless as a monkey on a bicycle (though not as entertaining). This does not mean you should crudely bolt a contrived storyline onto the real substance of the brochure. It means you should identify a theme derived from the brochure's key marketing message and use it to underpin each page.

Pristine Cleaners, an office cleaning company, know that their potential customers are looking for something more fresh and modern than the old-fashioned 'Mrs Mop' type of cleaner, and they have modelled their business around providing such a service.

Their brochure has the theme of 'Fresh Thinking' running throughout it. Every page tackles a key concern of potential clients – such as capability, dependability and security – and in each case it reveals the contemporary methods they use to ensure an effective solution.

What help do you need?

A corporate brochure is not usually something you can prepare, write, design and print yourself. It requires outside assistance. Either a graphic designer and a printer, or an all-in-one design & print service.

Get your designer and printer on board right from the beginning, so they are in the loop and available to liaise with you from the outset.

» Graphic design

The designer's involvement may include anything from improving presentation and instilling the company's brand to arranging photography and preparing files for the printer. Unless your business is opting for a very basic arrangement, this is not a job for an amateur.

A good designer is one that has proven experience and asks about the precise purpose of the brochure, who the target readership is and how you want them to respond. A designer that is happy to just plonk everything down onto a page regardless of these issues is not a real designer – they are just someone who knows how to use the software.

» Printing

There are many forms a corporate brochure can take, ranging from the conventional booklet to folders that contain a collection of inserts dependent on the needs of each recipient. And there are plenty of companies around that will print it for you, each with their own specialism: limited colour work, multi-colour work; small paper sizes, large paper sizes; small quantities, large quantities… and so on.

After discussing your brochure's content, particularly any photographs or graphic elements, as well as your budget, the printer will be able to offer advice on which paper is best for your needs. Make sure you get to see samples and a dummy copy of the entire brochure before giving the go-ahead for the full print run.

Dumplings

The Japanese have a saying:

HANA YORI DANGO

(Dumplings rather than flowers)

Just as when your stomach is rumbling, you need food, your prospective readers are hungry for something too. So you should give it to them. No amount of gimmickry or decoration will compensate if they are not getting what they want.

Never sacrifice content for the sake of appearance. Designers and printers are there to strengthen your marketing message. It is essential, therefore, that all presentation and production work is tackled with the same customer-centric rigour as all other stages in the preparation of your brochure.

❸ TONE OF VOICE

As you read this book, do you want to read all about me? Of course not. That would be irrelevant to the solutions you seek – and it would be tedious (I am a very boring person).

Likewise, readers of a corporate brochure do not want to read about the business. They want solutions to their needs. Which is why your brochure should be personal, not corporate.

It's okay to be informal

When some people write a corporate brochure, their normal conversational style of communication switches to the kind of stiff, formal language you would expect the Governor of the Bank of England to use when he is writing a report for the Chancellor of the Exchequer. Remember, you need to speak your readers' language. Relax, be yourself, have fun – and your writing will come across as clear, simple and enjoyable to read.

As well as making things nicer for your readers, using simple, accessible language makes things easier for you, as you can write like a human being instead of a robot.

A conversational tone encourages a response, as if the reader is taking part in a dialogue (how they actually respond will be discussed later in this chapter).

CORPORATE:

The manufacturing process results in a curtailment of unnecessary outlay. See fig 7.9 for an illustration.

PERSONAL:

By cutting waste we cut costs, and then we pass the savings on to you.

Empathise

You won't impress anyone if you pack the brochure with self-absorbed, self-aggrandising self-praise written from the business owner's perspective. Whether you are referring to the company's products, services, ethos or achievements, structure the content to express how it benefits the reader.

Think of the prospective customer. Feel their pain. Then tell them how you can help.

CORPORATE:

Our products are of a high quality.

PERSONAL:

Nothing wastes time and money like {their problem}. Now you can overcome this thanks to {your solution}.

Talk to the reader

This may seem obvious, but a great many brochures use language that appears to be talking to someone else. They talk about the reader as if they had not been invited to the discussion.

Address your customer directly, as if they were sat in front of you.

CORPORATE:

Customers' needs are assessed immediately in order to provide them with a rapid response.

PERSONAL:

We assess your needs immediately so we can provide you with a rapid response.

Use your native tongue

Using jargon when speaking to a person unfamiliar with that particular brand of lingo makes you sound like someone who (a) can't speak English properly and (b) can't express what you do in simple language. Unless you can be certain that your prospective clients are au fait with your jargon, you may as well write your brochure in Swahili.

> *Don't let language obstruct the message*
> Write to impress the reader, not the people who work in the business.

Use simple, commonly understood English.

CORPORATE:

The PHP WebSockets server released under a BSD-style open source licence has been actualised to identify additional capital resources among existing models.

PERSONAL:

This software is cheaper to use.

Be upfront

Using the third person (he, she, them) sounds like someone else has written your brochure. A client wants to know you are being upfront, so use the first person (I, we) when talking about the company.

Write like it's a personal correspondence with a client.

CORPORATE:

The company's meticulous approach sets them apart from the competition.

PERSONAL:

Our meticulous approach sets us apart from others.

Write like you mean it

Wishy washy sentences just make you appear half-hearted. To avoid this impression your language needs to convey a sense of action. You can do this by using active sentences – where the dynamic form of the verb is placed near the front of the sentence.

Say what you *will* do, not what will be done.

CORPORATE:

Your offices will be cleaned by our staff.

PERSONAL:

We will clean your office.

❹ CONTENT

Tempting though it is to chuck in everything there is to know about the business, the corporate brochure should be thought of as an introduction rather than a comprehensive and detailed report.

Think of it like a first date. If you launch into a detailed lecture on your auntie's gallstone operation, the prospects of a second date are not good. Knowing what to say and when to say it will give the reader a taste of why they should find out more.

Front cover headline

The front cover is the only page in the brochure that no one can avoid seeing. Therefore, it is the best opportunity you've got to get your key message across to the reader.

A headline promising a key benefit can excite the reader and entice them to turn the page and read on. It is more important than the company name and the company logo. It is so important that, without a wow-inducing headline, most people won't bother opening the brochure at all. So what should this all-important headline say?

Tell the reader, in just a few words, that you can address their needs like nobody else can

Simple as that. Remember, it's just a headline, not an advertisement. So state how you are the answer the readers' prayers and leave the rest for the inside pages.

Agrow Chemicals, a manufacturer of agricultural weed killers, uses the headline:

We'll make your profits grow, not weeds

Cake Craft, a supplier of cake decorations, uses the headline:

Everything you need for creative baking

Front cover image

Although a picture is more appealing than a plain cover, be careful to avoid nondescript images, such as a picture of your premises, and do not simply repeat the headline in a crude visual way. Instead, put an image on the front cover that lets readers know immediately what the brochure is all about.

The image should expand on the promise of the headline

Rather than showing a container full of some highly toxic substance, Agrow Chemicals, the manufacturer of agricultural weed killer, shows the chemicals being applied safely and easily via one of their impressive-looking spraying machines.

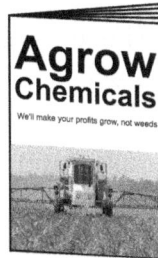

Agrow Chemicals
We'll make your profits grow, not weeds

Rather than simply displaying their products, Cake Craft, uses an eye-catching image of a multi-tiered cake stand filled with beautifully decorated cupcakes.

Cake Craft

Everything you need for creative baking

Introduction

As soon as they open the brochure, you need to have your stall set out to show customers exactly what you have to offer. Whether this takes the form of a straightforward piece of introductory text or a letter from the head honcho, it needs to be fresh and minimal. Nobody wants to turn to page 1 and be faced with a page full of waffle to plough through. Hone it so there is nothing superfluous, vague or uninspiring in there.

Your introduction should express:

1   The problem the reader faces

2   The solution you provide

Depending on the company's line of business, the 'problem' could be anything from paying the mortgage:

> These days it's hard to predict what will happen to our finances…

To dressing a Chihuahua:

> These days, it's hard to find small dog clothes that are both practical and fashionable…

The 'solution' you promise should be something specific to your business, that sets you apart from the competition and sets the scene for the rest of the brochure.

> …a personal service that combines free financial advice with a range of dependable investments.

> …a pooch pampering service that combines bespoke tailoring with a range of doggy designer accessories.

Although it is not an 'about us' section, you can incorporate company profile details in your introduction, as long as it is tailored towards how it benefits the customer.

A clothes designer combines business information, the customers' problem, the solution, and a meaningful narrative all in one introduction:

> Recognising how difficult it is for women of a certain age to find the right sports clothes, I decided to confront the problem by designing my own.
>
> That was in 2002, and now my range of practical and flattering sportswear has increased to include...

Products and services

Your corporate brochure is an opportunity to showcase your distinctive products and services – as long as it is written within the framework of how they help readers meet the challenges that face them. Do not try to mention every product and service, that will alienate anyone who has no interest in some of what you have to offer. Leave details about prices, specifications and ordering for the sales brochure (see the Product Descriptions chapter). Here you only need to answer the readers' central concern:

How does your product/service affect me?

The answer is not something about the product:

> The FX-90 is 30% faster than the TZ-50

It is about how this benefits the reader:

> Enjoy 30% more free time

If there are different groups of clients that you want to tailor the brochure towards, you could always insert individual loose product sheets into the brochure to cater for their specific needs, or go for the folder style of brochure where it is entirely comprised of a selection of loose sheets.

Prove your pudding

It is nice to suppose that anyone taking a look at your brochure will be doing so with a rose-tinted perspective, all thoughts of cynicism put well and truly aside. All the same, you should prepare for less trusting readers who want to see some actual evidence.

Support any claims you make in the brochure with hard facts, statistics and any other proof you can muster

Whatever evidence you manage to assemble, it not only strengthens your case, it serves to break up the inevitable 'me me me' nature of the brochure with an outsider's perspective.

» Case studies

Real life examples of how your business has solved a customer's problem. It does not have to be an entire case study, you can just cut and paste the key points. If you haven't got any case studies to cut and paste from, then create a summary of a job you have successfully undertaken, giving all names, dates and details of the problem and how you solved it.

» Testimonials

Quotes from past clients stating how their concerns were addressed with expertise, professionalism and gusto. The more unequivocal facts and figures included the better.

» Press cuttings

Any third party recognition of what a business is capable of carries more weight than anything they could say themselves. So whether the company gets a favourable mention in The Times, the Bolton Evening News or the Button Suppliers' Gazette, put a clipping in the brochure.

Encourage a response

What's the point in creating the perfect corporate brochure, then not telling the reader what to do next? Without this vital piece of direction, what else is the reader expected to do other than put the brochure down and forget about it?

At the end of the brochure, possibly on the back cover itself, you need to do two things.

1   Provide the full contact details:

Phone number, email address, website address, business address, social media usernames...

2   Tell the reader precisely what to do:

Call for a chat; visit a website; visit a shop; place an order; tear off an attached strip and send off for a no obligation consultation...

Don't be shy. This isn't aggressive selling, this is a natural conclusion to what you have just spent the whole brochure leading towards.

Back cover

Depending on which way your brochure is picked up or put down, it could have the wrong side facing up. So don't give it a 'wrong' side:

Treat the back cover like another front cover

The back cover should provide sufficient information to convey in an instant what the brochure is all about. For example:

- *O* A repeat of the front cover headline
- *O* An image that corresponds with the image on the front cover

It could be used as a place to present obligatory information:

- *O* Contact details
- *O* Company name and logo

It is also a prime spot to locate any impressive third party corroboration:

- *O* A particularly compelling testimonial
- *O* Details of any awards that have been received

Don't feel that you have to have all of these things squashed onto your back cover. Just select what is most appropriate for the type of business and style of brochure.

Avoid obsolescence

If you want your corporate brochure to be around for some time, be careful not to limit its lifespan by including anything that could put it out of date prematurely:

- *O* A profile of a star member of staff – who might leave to work for a competitor

- *O* A product launch – that might be cancelled

- *O* A location map – prior to a move to new premises

- *O* A reference to the latest fad or a topical news event – that soon becomes yesterday's news

- *O* Any phrases such as, "The research programme began 7 years ago" – replace with future-proof wording like, "The research programme began in 2010"

Of course, your corporate brochure cannot last forever. But with a little forethought, it need not experience an early demise.

❺ PRESENTATION

While you may be thinking that every turn of the page presents an enthusiastic readership with another piece of eagerly sought after information, the readership see things quite differently. For them, each new page is an opportunity to stop reading.

That is why you must present the brochure in a way that continually catches the reader's eye and entices them to read on.

Images

Visuals are the first thing the reader sees when they turn over to a new page. They should work in tandem with the accompanying text. A good picture can say a thousand words. So can a bad picture – all of them unflattering.

Here are the rules for images:

- ✗ Don't include images just for the sake of it
- ✓ Each picture should serve a purpose, showing the reader something relevant to their needs
- ✗ Don't use clichéd corporate photos: a woman answering a phone, a close up shot of a handshake, a computer keyboard etc.
- ✓ Think what you want your image to say and say it in a fresh, original way that comes from you, not a stock photo library
- ✗ Don't use a picture of your building
- ✓ Unless your premises are particularly distinctive, or unless they are part of what you are selling in some way (such as a café), the building is something for your benefit, not your customers'

Captions

Once you have images that convey something worthwhile to your prospective readers, you should write captions for them. Captions are among the first things people read when they flick through a brochure, so use them to reiterate your key selling points.

> Confetti Wedding Planners include a lovely picture of an old Rolls Royce Silver Ghost. Beneath it is the caption: 'The car of your wedding dreams is yours for the day'.

Centre spread

It is well known, in brochure design circles, that the middle pages of any brochure – the centre spread – possess a power beyond that of any of the preceding or following pages.

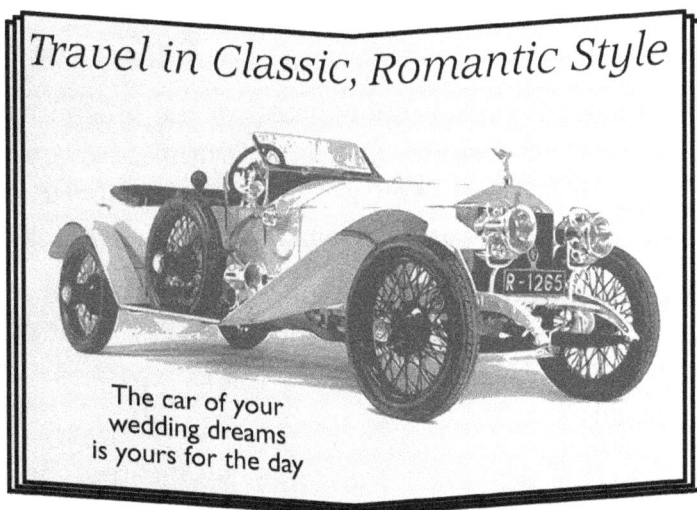

Travel in Classic, Romantic Style

The car of your wedding dreams is yours for the day

There are three reasons for this:

1   It is the only part of the brochure where the left and right hand pages come into perfect alignment (because they are, in fact, a single sheet of paper).

2   If a reader were to open the brochure at a random page, just to get a feel for what it's about, they would most likely find themselves looking at the centre spread.

3   The ideal moment at which to surprise browsers with something a bit different to look at is midway through the brochure.

The centre spread provides a once-in-a-brochure opportunity to break free from the strictures of the single page and run headlines, pictures, tables and charts across the fold without the familiar fissure running through it, or worse, the page-tectonic shift, sending everything out of kilter as you cross from one page to the next.

Scannability

After you have collated the content for the brochure, read over it for the umpteenth time, and scrutinised every word and punctuation mark, you are no longer seeing it as the person who will be reading it for the first time will see it.

At best, they will be reading it quickly, most likely they will be reading it too fast to take in most of what they see. So you need to think of your brochure in this way, and make it easy to scan.

You can do this in two ways. First, by incorporating key messages in a variety of places other than the main body of writing, like this...

Headlines: The one line on a page that can't help but be read.

Give each page a clear benefit as a headline. As the reader moves through the brochure the headlines will build on the brochure's theme, offering a progression with growing impact.

Subheads: More than just a description of what's coming next, subheads can shout out key benefits.

Panels

A detached box showing separate, related, information.

Call-outs

Short text descriptions with a line or arrow pointing to the relevant part of an image.

Captions *Impossible not to read when you see the image*

The second way to improve scannability is to make longer pieces of text shorter and easier to read. Before reading a piece of text, a person makes a subconscious decision: 'Do I want to bother embarking on this potentially demoralising experience?'.

Here are some ways to avoid this potential pitfall...

Separate paragraphs with photographs and other visuals to ensure there are no large solid blocks of text.

Keep paragraphs and sentences short and simple, so that words fall into the reader's mind without any mental exertion.

~ ~ ~

Use an easily-readable font for the text throughout the brochure, and make it large enough to be read by anyone over the age of 40. Remember, you are not designing it for you, you are designing it for your reader, who may need reading glasses.

Don't allow lines of text to stretch, unabated, across the page. Keep them contained within columns of a manageable width.

Lead the eye to where the you want it to begin reading. You can do this using devices like large initial capital letters and **bold** lettering.

Follow these guidelines and a reader will be able to take in almost your entire brochure with just a quick scan.

As the French mathematician and philosopher, Blaise Pascal, wrote in one of his correspondences: "If I had more time, I would have written a shorter letter."

Blaise Pascal, 1623 - 1662

That is, it takes more effort to create a succinct message that carries weight than a long-winded exposition that no one can be bothered to read. So cut out the flannel and make sure that every word counts.

BUSINESS CARDS

**Create a mini masterpiece that
makes a big impression**

Most business cards are about as much use as a scrap of paper with a name and number scribbled on it. That's fine if you are looking for a date, but not so good for showcasing a business.

This chapter shows you how to create a business card that packs a promotional punch and generates interest like it were fifty pound notes you were handing over.

What's in this Chapter?

❶ CARDIOLOGY

Imagine that an entire business was distilled, desiccated, flattened and shaped so that every detail of what they do and how they do it was encapsulated in a wafer-thin, palm-sized rectangle of card.

The intense power of such a card belies its meagre proportions, and it continues to trump other, more modern, methods of saying: "Hello".

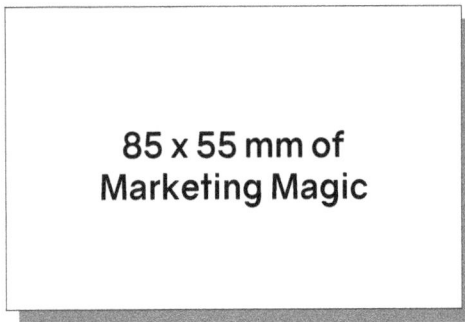

**85 x 55 mm of
Marketing Magic**

Apart from being the embodiment of simple elegance, bolstering your confidence with a sense of professionalism, and giving you a warm fuzzy feeling when you pick them up from the printers, business cards are...

» Fast

Slip someone your business card and you give them an instant insight into your business.

» Tenacious

Like a tiny salesperson that sticks with your prospective client, your card works hard on your behalf long after you have parted company.

» Universal

There are no compatibility problems, no registering your details and no batteries required. Your card can be understood by anyone.

» Individual

Your business's entire ethos and personality is contained on your card. It is as unique as you are.

» Friendly

Exchanging business cards has a ritual significance that heralds the start of a convivial relationship.

» Convenient

It fits between a thumb and forefinger and slips effortlessly into a pocket or wallet.

» Targeted

It enables a one-to-one marketing opportunity with a captive audience.

» Handy

You can have them on you at all times, hand them out when you meet others, leave them where people will see them and slip them in with any correspondence.

» Cheap

Like all design classics and time-honoured marketing techniques, business cards won't cost you a fortune.

② CONTENT

On the following pages you will find all the things you can consider putting on a business card, along with advice on how to deploy them.

A business card does not have to include everything that is covered in this section. Too much information is as bad as not enough. So just select the elements that suit the nature of the business, the target audience and the objectives for the card.

Identity

The name of the business, the individual and their job title may seem pretty straightforward, but it still needs a bit of thought about how the information will be prioritised. The trick is to put yourself in the mind of the person you are giving the card to.

Emphasise what is most important to the recipient

Wendy Barker's graphic design business, Imaginings, has six different ways to prioritise their key information:

Wendy Barker	**Wendy Barker**	**Imaginings Ltd**
Imaginings Ltd	Graphic Design	Graphic Design
Graphic Design	Imaginings Ltd	Wendy Barker
Imaginings Ltd	**Graphic Design**	**Graphic Design**
Wendy Barker	Imaginings Ltd	Wendy Barker
Graphic Design	Wendy Barker	Imaginings Ltd

As Wendy is handing out cards to local businesses in the hope that they will use her when there is graphic design to be done, it is the words 'Graphic Design' that need to resonate with the client. This does not necessarily mean it should be at the top, but it should be the first thing that catches the eye. In this case, the remaining two elements can have equal status.

Wendy Barker

GRAPHIC DESIGN

Imaginings Ltd

Then you may wish to add a job title into the mix. With larger companies, of course, clients like to know the position of the person they are dealing with, but with start-ups, sole traders and some small businesses, the job title may be unnecessary, or at least relegated to a minor supporting role.

Your card is not about you
The recipient isn't interested whether you call yourself CEO, Global Director or Generalissimo in Charge of Absolutely Everything – all they want to know is what you can do for them.

Contact

Office telephone number, mobile telephone number, fax number, e-mail address, website address, street address, LinkedIn, Twitter, Facebook, Instagram... nowadays you could fill an A4 sheet with contact details.

You need to minimise any clutter on the card, so think: does anyone care about your old MySpace page or even, for that matter, the address of your office?

Only include contact details that people want

What the recipient of the card wants may be minimal:

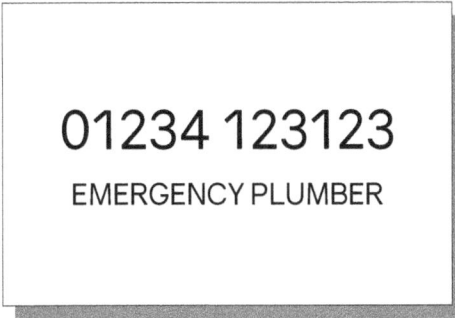

01234 123123
EMERGENCY PLUMBER

Or, if social media forms a key part of the business, it may be more widespread:

email:	john.collins@channelxmedia.com
tel:	01234 123123
mob:	07654 321321
twitter:	ChannelXmedia
linkedIn:	ChannelXmedia
facebook:	ChannelXmedia
web:	ChannelXmedia.com
blog:	ChannelXmedia.com/blog

Tagline

As well as providing the essentials, a business card should differentiate the holder from the rest of the crowd. You can do this with a tagline. This doesn't necessarily mean reproducing your company slogan.

Tailor your tagline to the card's objectives

The tagline can take the form of:

» A prompt

A sandwich bar hands out cards to people working in nearby offices with the following inducement:

> Need a sandwich?
>
> Call now and you'll have it in 10mins

» A reason to make contact

An IT support company hands out cards carrying an enticing incentive:

> Free consultation with this card

» A way to usher the reader elsewhere

A clothes designer knows that the images on her website are her greatest sales asset:

> Visit
>
> KidsKlothes.com
>
> for latest designs

» An indication of your ethos

An interior design service indicates their determination to bring out clients' own personal style with the quote:

> "Be faithful to your own taste,
>
> because nothing you really like
>
> is ever out of style"

» Whatever gives you the competitive edge

In an industry where standard office hours are the norm, this tagline sets one business apart from the competition:

> Evening and weekend
>
> appointments available

Blurb

Simply stating the nature of your business is not always enough.

Explain where you are coming from

For instance, it may be advantageous to clarify whether you are a global conglomerate or a local newcomer; an all-embracing one-stop-shop or a slimmed-down outsourcer of services.

A manufacturer of vehicle components spells out exactly what it does:

> Using high-pressure die casting, squeeze casting and vacuum / pressure riserless casting to produce parts for the chassis, suspension, engine and driveline systems.

An interior design company differentiates itself from other interior design companies by adding:

> With 25 years' experience and a large portfolio of clients, Squires Interiors undertakes residential and commercial commissions throughout the UK and overseas.

Services

Unlike in a brochure or on a website where you have room to elaborate, a business card's list of products or services needs to be short and simple, no matter how numerous they are.

Turn a long list into a punchy précis

A copywriting company lists the following services on its website:

advertising	mailshots
articles	marketing
blogs	newsletters
brochures	online marketing
business writing	press releases
case studies	sales letters
catalogues	search engine optimisation
direct mail	websites
leaflets & flyers	

But on their business card, this list is reduced to four core headings:

Websites | Brochures | Advertising | Editorial

Images

If the visual aspect of what you do is important when drumming up new customers, put it on your card.

Show off your work

A wedding photographer with a distinctive style communicates this by using almost his entire business card to display a sample photograph:

Testimonials

If a business is reliant on recommendations, reproducing a testimonial from a well known client on the card will spread the word to the people that matter.

Give word of mouth a hand

If there are not any good testimonial ready to use, write your own, then ask the client for permission to attribute it to them. They will probably enjoy the free publicity it gives them.

An event organiser uses the following quote to demonstrate their credentials:

> *"The vintage car show you held in our grounds was an absolute triumph"*
>
> *Bricknell Hall, Wiltshire*

A firm of decorators wishing to expand into corporate work uses this testimonial on their card:

> *"A first class job with minimal disruption"*
>
> *Forbes Hotel, York*

Clients

With some industries, if you want to land a contract you need to communicate that you have solid experience.

Add the proof of the pudding

A list of past clients can do this, especially if they are recognisable and verifiable.

A web design company, aiming to show potential clients that they are not just a spotty 14 year old working from a computer in their bedroom, lists the web addresses of past clients. This not only provides company names, it allows people to visit the sites and view the work for themselves.

A company providing training for businesses wishing to attract more retail clients includes the following on its card:

> Existing clients: Asda, Boots, Next

Availability

If it is important for customers to know when a company is open for business...

State your opening times

A chiropodist uses a simple table to provide the essential information customers need:

Mon–Fri	10 am – 7 pm
Saturday	12 noon – 4 pm
Sunday	closed

A yoga centre gives details of class times:

Beginners:
Mon 6pm ~ Tues 8pm ~ Wed 8pm

Improvers:
Mon 8pm ~ Tues 7pm ~ Sat 9am

Advanced:
Tues 6pm ~ Wed 6pm ~ Sat 10am

Map

If a business wants customers to beat a path to their door, customers need to know how to find their way.

Make it easy to be found

A beautician based some way off the High Street helps new customers find their way to the studio with this simple map:

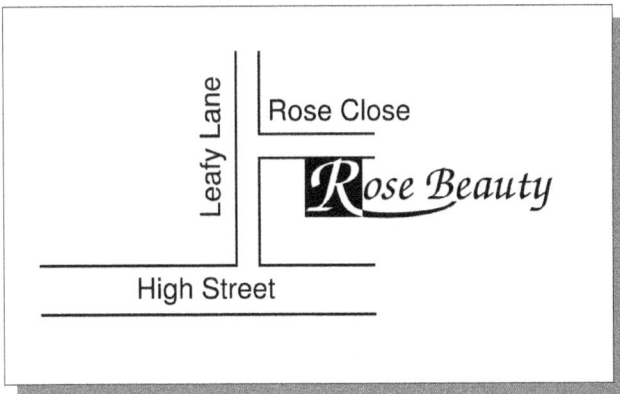

A distribution centre for an online retailer provides a handy guide to their location:

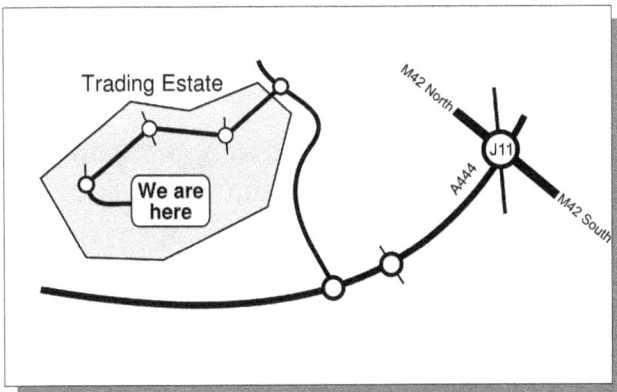

Branding

Add a logo, if there is one, and any other distinctive elements from the business's identity, such as colour, graphics, font and so on.

Use a coherent identity across all stationary

A consistent identity that encompasses the business card, letterhead, complement slip, invoice, quotation and everything else relating to the business tells prospective customers that they are a professional outfit with a clear and consistent vision of what they are about.

QR Code

A QR Code (Quick Response Code) is a square barcode that can be read using smartphones and the like.

Once scanned by the recipient it can, for example, add all the contact information to their address book or take them to a specific landing page on the company website. If a business deals with the type of people that would scan a QR Code, then it is an easy way to add an extra dimension to the card. Just make sure that the outcome of the code isn't an anti-climax.

Use the QR code for a worthwhile purpose

A designer of expensive wedding dresses knows that clients will not use her without checking out her work beforehand, so she makes it easy for them to do this by putting a scannable link on her business card.

If a business has pages on their website featuring 'special offers', a QR code can be generated for each individual offer and used to gather valuable marketing data. This could be expanded across a variety of media. For example, one QR code could be for posters in a High Street shop, another could be used on leaflets pushed through letterboxes, and so on.

To discover how to create a code that will do your bidding, Google 'QR code generator' and you will be rewarded with a plethora of websites offering to do it for you.

❸ PRESENTATION

A smart, well-expressed card says a lot about you and your business – as does a vague and confused one. So, how do you want to be perceived?

Check out the following character traits and suggestions for how to ensure your business's personality shines out from every card.

Clear and to the point

People do not want to wade through lots of wordy clutter when you hand them your business card. It needs to convey its message with instant impact, like a huge advertising hoarding, but with pocket-sized proportions.

- ⊘ Check that all the information you have collated for use on the card is strictly necessary (think: will the recipient be pleased to have it?). Then arrange it in a logical and legible manner, prioritised according to its importance to the person it is to be handed to.

- ⊘ Choose your font with care. Despite what I said about adding branding to your content, sometimes you need to adapt fonts to suit the size of the card. Whichever font you choose, make sure it looks professional. I like Century Gothic, because of its clarity and rounded 'a' (most fonts use the more elaborate 'a'), you may prefer Garamond for its traditional feel. Experiment and see which font suits your business and your message best.

Wendy Barker
GRAPHIC DESIGN

Imaginings Ltd	07777 777777
27 High Street	wendy@imaginings.com
Town on Sea	www.imaginings.com

Leaflets | Business cards | Websites | Logos

Lots of information presented with absolute clarity

Understated and elegant

Having more stuff on your card doesn't make your card more impressive. In fact, the opposite is usually the case.

℗ Make room for empty space. Empty space gives your information prominence. So add lots of it. It also leaves room for notes: people often write on cards, such as a reminder to give you a call.

℗ If you are short of space, one way to create more of it is to use both sides of the card. De-cluttering your card will give your main message more impact.

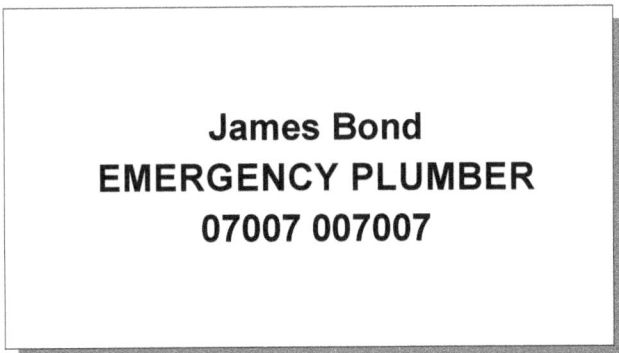

James Bond
EMERGENCY PLUMBER
07007 007007

Understated, elegant and licensed to plumb

Full of fun

If you want to give a business card something extra, so that it not only stands out from the dross but grabs the recipient's attention like it was a lighted stick of dynamite you had just handed over, you may wish to consider a gimmick of some sort.

ⓔ Something that opens up, pops out or incorporates origami in some way or other can make a card stand out, but make sure you choose something relevant to the aims of your card.

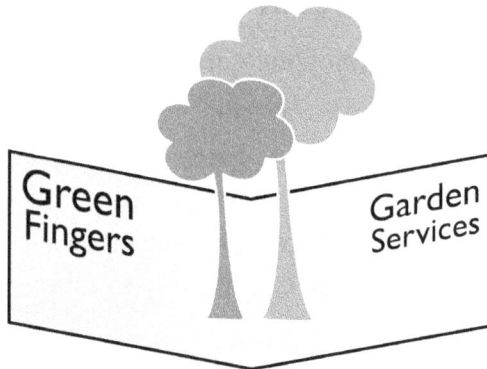

*An unforgettable marketing message, or
a short-lived plaything?*

Although very popular, diverging from the 'information presented clearly on a rectangle of card' way of doing things is usually a bad idea. People want clear information, not to be entertained. Having an unusual card may initially catch people's eyes, but the novelty soon wears off, especially when it won't fit into a standard card holder or wallet.

Not black and white

Business cards don't have to be monochrome. Colours can be used as a kind of shorthand to describe your business. But only use colour for a purpose, not just for the sake of it. Otherwise you cross the line into gimmick territory.

Bright bold colours convey the right image for a funky, young TV production company.

Heritage colours communicate a feeling of age-old quality for an antique dealer.

A good place to get ideas for colours is to pick up some paint sample charts from your local DIY store. A professional printer can also advise you on 'Pantone colours', which guarantee colour consistency across all of your printed marketing materials.

Serious and professional

If someone greets you with a handshake like a limp lettuce it leaves you with the impression that they are lacking in something. The same is true of business cards. Hand someone a flimsy card and you appear flimsy yourself. Similarly, they won't thank you if you hand them a card that cuts through their jacket pocket like a piece of honed steel.

    Ø To use printers' terminology, you should go for 300gsm stock for your business cards. This level of stiffness lies pleasantly in-between the extremes and has a nice feeling of quality about it. Ask your printer to show you the card beforehand so you can feel it for yourself (remembering that a large sheet will feel more flexible than a small business card).

Talking of printers, after all this thought and attention to detail, it would be a shame to ruin the card with poor production.

- Choose a print company with a good digital colour machine that can handle 300gsm stock or heavier. You may also want to enquire if they can offer letterpress printing. This creates an embedded impression of your text in the card, giving it a deeply inked and luxurious tactile quality.

- The printer will advise on all the practicalities, such as the file format to provide the data in (this can vary depending on whether it is text, graphics, photography and so on) and whether you should allow for bleed (artwork extending beyond the actual boundaries of the card).

- Finally, before giving the go-ahead, ask for a test print, or proof, so you can see, for the first time, how the real thing actually looks.

EMAILS

Create inbox-friendly communications

Anyone at all active online will be familiar with email marketing: automated sales emails that bombard our inboxes with all the subtlety and sensitivity of a brick through the window.

Occasionally, however, more agreeable emails arrive, making a genuinely useful proposition. These are rewarded by being read and, perhaps, receiving a reply.

This chapter is about writing those kind of emails.

WHAT'S IN THIS CHAPTER?

❶ HOW TO NOT BE SPAMMY

Offer steak to a man that has been fed spam all his life and he will devour it with gusto – and want to know if there's more where that came from.

Unfortunately, like a good steak, appetising marketing emails are rare. Even so, here are two ways to ensure you always serve up enticing prime cuts that are 100% spam-free.

The personal-yet-business-generating email

Amid the onslaught of bulk-mailed, one-size-fits-all templates that clog up the world's email system, the business email that stands out from the clutter is the one that looks like it has been written specifically for the person receiving it (however many people it has been sent to).

Here's how to give your email the personal touch:

» Introduce, don't sell

Restrict your message to an introduction rather than an attempt to ambush the hapless reader with a full-scale sales pitch. The aim is to whet the reader's appetite, not force feed them information like a foie gras goose.

» Build a relationship

Imagine the recipient is sat at the other side of your desk. If you spout off about yourself incessantly they will soon lose interest. If you treat them as part of a homogeneous group rather than as an individual, they will think you are ignorant. Instead, seek to empathise with their specific concerns and build a personal relationship based on a shared interest.

» Keep it simple

Make it easy on the eye. Don't clutter your message with different coloured text, mixed fonts, capital letters, highlighting, bold, exclamation marks etc. Stick with a 'sans serif' font such as Arial, or possibly a 'typewriter' or 'serif' font such as Times, but never, God forbid, Comic Sans. Personally, I like Verdana. It gives more space around each letter, making the words seem less cramped.

» Don't include images

You need to make your case using words, not pictures that most people will be unable to see anyway because they are blocked by any half-decent security software.

» Keep it short

If an unexpected email is to be read, it needs to be short enough for the reader to see at a glance what it is about. Something around 150-200 words should be ample.

The promotional-yet-not-pushy email

Of course, it is possible to be salesy without being spammy. If you want to create emails that are more like advertisements for products or services, then please flick forward a few pages to the 'Sales Letters' chapter. Here you will find exactly what you require, but in an offline form.

To email-ify it, simply use the letter headline as your email subject line. The rest is the same and will result in a sales email that is promotional, but not pushy.

Oh, and remember, if you are intending to repeatedly email someone, it must be permission-based.

② THE MESSAGE

Your email may contain the most thrilling proposition since The Fish Marketing Board decided to get in touch with The Chips Association, but unless you can communicate it in an effortlessly accessible fashion, no one is going to spend valuable seconds of their life reading it.

Fortunately, there is a method that helps you convey your proposal with almost telepathic ease.

What you are really saying

Each element of your message has a distinct function, which can be summarised like this:

```
Hello
It's OK, I'm not spam.
I know your business.
I understand your concerns.
I can help.
Have no doubt.
See for yourself.
It couldn't be easier.
Cheerio
```

How to create the actual wording for each element is explained in the following pages, and a complete example is provided at the end of this chapter.

'Hello'

You should certainly use the recipient's name (begin with 'Dear Sir/Madam' and you may as well delete it before you press send – it'll save the recipient time). It is just a choice between:

1. Hi {first name},

2. Dear {first name},

3. Dear {title and surname},

You need to make a judgement about which is most appropriate for the prospective reader. It is something that depends to a large degree on the industry and the age of the recipient.

'It's OK, I'm not spam'

This is the biggy. What you say in the opening sentence tells the reader what kind of message it is: just another piece of junk, or something of real interest.

> *The first objective of any email*
> Dispel the reader's natural assumption that you are trying to sell to them or con them in some way.

To differentiate your email from indiscriminate spam you need to convey that it is a personal correspondence from someone who knows the recipient's business and has something genuine to say – all in one short sentence.

To accomplish this, we use algebra:

Opening sentence = x, but y + z

Where:

x= A humble acknowledgement that it's a bit of a cheek intruding on their inbox.

y= Flattery about them and their work.

z= Reassurance that you will take up barely any of their valuable time.

Simply substitute in the values for x, y and z and, hey presto, you have a cracker of an opening sentence. It's a mathematical fact.

A graphic designer approaches a small company producing smoothies using a suitably informal style:

> I know you're very busy, but I love the use of design on all your packaging and I'd like to ask a quick question if I may?

Pole Position, a Polish-English business translation service, begin their message to the marketing manager of Agrimatic, a local agricultural manufacturer exporting to Poland, with the following opener:

> I hope you don't mind me contacting you directly, but as the person responsible for getting Agrimatic's message across, I'd appreciate a minute of your time.

'I know your business'

Boasting of your prowess across a broad range of sectors will mean less to your reader than something that is specific and relevant to them.

Refer to any projects, clients, individuals, events etc. that demonstrate a common bond with the prospect. This is the sort of thing that will resonate with them and establish a rapport between the two of you.

A business consultant says to his prospect in the oil industry:

> As I work a lot within the Chemical, Oil & Gas industry, I am very familiar with your company's activities in the North Sea.

Pole Position bonds with Agrimatic's marketing manager by demonstrating a knowledge of the company's activities as well as personal insight:

> I understand that your company is making inroads into the Polish agricultural sector. As a Pole myself, I am very familiar with this potentially huge market.

'I understand your concerns'

Now you need to get straight to the point and address the issue at hand. But remember, the issue is not about your offer – it is about their concerns.

What need of theirs are you aiming to satisfy? A simple way to bring up their concerns is with a question.

A waste recycling company addresses their prospect's needs like this:

```
Are you managing to cut the waste your
business produces, or will you be facing
the huge fines set by the EU Landfill
Directive?
```

Pole Position focuses the reader's mind by asking a question:

```
I was wondering, do you have the time and
expertise to accurately translate your
marketing material to fully exploit this
opportunity?
```

'I can help'

Tell them how you will make their life better. What benefits will they enjoy by dealing with you? Provide evidence if possible.

Don't get ahead of yourself by compelling the reader to sign on the dotted line. The aim is to initiate the process. For this reason, whether your business provides products or services, as far as the email is concerned, you are simply making an offer of assistance.

A company producing uniforms and specialist work clothing does not send out emails that look like a product page from its catalogue – it sends out emails explaining what they do, emphasising the customer-benefits with the aim of moving things along to the point where the reader will ask to see samples and prices.

Pole Position follows on from raising the issue of marketing translation to emphasising their expertise in this area – and backing it up with a real-life success story:

> The reason I ask is, my company, Pole Position, has helped clients such as Dawson Electronics achieve success in Poland. Our specialist translators understand the subtleties of marketing language, so your sales message is never lost in translation.

'Have no doubt'

Tackle any resistance head-on. You haven't the luxury of time to deal with questions later on, you need to defuse their objections before they even arise.

A commercial blog writing business, based in the north of Scotland, sends emails across the UK to drum up business. Anticipating that they might be rejected because of their remote location, they make a virtue of it:

> Working via email and telephone is faster and it keeps costs down.

Pole Position are aware that their small size and provincial location could deter prospective clients. Instead of trying to hide it, they use it to their advantage:

> With all the skills and professionalism of a large agency, we also give you the personal attention that only a small, local company can provide.

'See for yourself'

Don't try to close the deal there and then. Expecting someone to commit themselves after a cursory glance at an unsolicited email is too much to ask. Just show the reader the way forward, by viewing samples of your work, for instance.

A web designer wants to urge prospects to see what he can do for them:

> If you take a quick look at my site (www.topnotch.net) you'll see that I can deliver smart e-commerce solutions for businesses very similar to yours.

Pole Position wants to encourage contact:

> You can see for yourself. Just let me know and I'll email across a few recent examples of our work along with client testimonials.
>
> Or, if you have a moment, I could call in any time and show you myself.

'It couldn't be easier'

A good way to neatly tie things up without losing the momentum you have gathered is to quickly follow on from suggesting the next step to telling them how to go about it.

Don't spoil it all by saying something stupid like: 'Call now!!!'. Stick with the obliging tone of the email and offer your contact details in a way that suggests it couldn't be easier, there's nothing to lose, so it's worth a shot.

A car valeting service looking to expand into the commercial sector ends with:

> So, why not give us a try? To discuss the details, see samples of our work or have a chat…

Pole position use:

> You can email me at vlatka@poleposition.com or call me on 06789 7654321.

'Cheerio'

The are four levels of sign-off, ranging from the formal to the easy-going. Again, it depends on the impression you want to give your reader.

1   Regards / Yours sincerely / Yours faithfully

2   Thank you

3   Best wishes

4   All the best / Thanks

Ending an email to a hip, youthful, digital arts enterprise, a data storage service signs off with:

> All the best,

Pole Position want to end like they began, appreciative of being given a moment of the reader's time:

```
Thank you,
Vlatka Komorowski
(Manager, Pole Position)
```

If you are part of a larger organisation, put your job title beneath your name. Alternatively, you may have a standard footer for your emails that includes your job title along with contact details.

Avoid the word 'Sales' in your job title as this would immediately negate the feeling of bonhomie that you have tried to build. 'Managing Director' or similar is best as it implies you are making a serious business proposition rather than simply selling something.

❸ FIRST IMPRESSIONS

Consider the initial impact your email will make on the unsuspecting recipient when it first materialises in their inbox.

The 'Subject' and 'From' lines are the only part of the email that the reader is guaranteed to see. And, after a split-second glance, they will decide whether your email is read or dead.

Subject

Write your subject line last, so that it accurately suggests the content of your message.

Look online and you will see plenty of information telling you how to craft 'killer' subject lines for marketing emails...

```
Are you missing out?
Today only: FREE Shipping!
Your personal invitation
You'll LOVE our new blinds!!
```

This kind of subject line is based on the presumption that your prospect has never received junk email before and will fall for any feeble attempt at hoodwinking them. What they see as an irresistible subject line, the rest of us see as 'DANGER: SPAM BOMB' and deal with it accordingly.

Let's assume instead that your prospect is a sensible person, well-versed in the wiles of junk mail. What kind of subject line would engage them enough to open an unexpected email? One that is...

» Relevant

Tap into what is on their mind. Something important to their work that is of genuine interest to them.

» Sincere

There is absolutely nothing to gain by misleading the reader.

» Short

Don't overcomplicate it. Just say what it is in as few words as possible.

» Unambiguous

An intriguing subject may cause some people to open an email, but an unequivocal one will generate actual responses.

» Personal

Your email is about the recipient and their needs. So there's no point putting, for example, the name of your company in your subject line.

» Hype-free

This doesn't mean you can't make a proposition or state a benefit. Just stick to the facts and avoid using capital letters and exclamation marks.

A freelance accountant emails small businesses using the subject line:

Subject:	Local accountant: I will save you money

This may seem too simple, but just imagine yourself as the owner of a small business who either lies awake at night worrying about finances or has to pay a firm of accountants a fortune to take care of it. A subject line that is personal and makes a genuine offer would surely prick your interest more than something like:

Subject:	SAVE £££s ON YOUR TAX BILL!!!

Simpler still, a photographer emails marketing managers with the subject line:

Subject:	Marketing photography

Again, it taps into precisely what the recipient is interested in and it doesn't look like a sales email, so it would most likely get opened. Whereas:

Subject:	Kick-Ass Photography

...would just result in a weary sigh and a swift drag to the delete folder.

From

When a recipient takes a quick look at who a newly arrived email is from they initially see the 'friendly' name. This can be configured before sending to display whatever you wish. On closer inspection, the actual email address can be determined.

In both cases, it is an opportunity to demonstrate to your prospect that you are not a corporate zombie, but a human being with whom they can relate.

Here are the options open to Dave Jones from WebTech web designers:

	Human Being	Corporate Zombie
Friendly name	Dave Jones	Sales
Actual address	d.jones@webtech.com	info@webtech.com

Would you rather receive an email from someone called 'Dave Jones', or from something called 'Sales'?

Test

Nothing scuppers an effective message quicker than a mistake. A single error will undo all your good work in an instant, so before you hit the send button, send a test email to a couple of colleagues. It will enable you to identify any problems with:

- Broken links. People are wary of clicking links at the best of times, so make sure yours work flawlessly.

- Dodgy formatting. The best advice is not to include any formatting other than plain text.

- Your email address. Does the 'friendly' name display as it should?

For added scrutiny, send to colleagues using different systems to yours. Then you can identify any discrepancies between Mac, PC and smartphone, and different types of email software.

A note about GDPR

GDPR (General Data Protection Regulation) is a set of rules created by the European Union to give consumers a greater say in how companies collect and use their data. Detailed information regarding the consequences of GDPR for email marketers is available online from many sources, including the UK's Information Commissioner's Office:

ico.org.uk

The key thing to remember is that the consumer must be fully aware of how and why their personal data will be used, and they should accept their approval by intentionally placing a checkmark in a subscription form to confirm they understand the terms and conditions and agree to receive your emails.

Subject: Polish marketing translation service

Dear Mr Howard,

I hope you don't mind me contacting you directly, but as the person responsible for getting Agrimatic's message across, I'd appreciate a minute of your time.

I understand that your company is making inroads into the Polish agricultural sector. As a Pole myself, I am very familiar with this potentially huge market.

I was wondering, do you have the time and expertise to accurately translate your marketing material to exploit this opportunity?

The reason I ask is, my company, Pole Position, has helped clients such as Dawson Electronics achieve success in Poland. Our specialist translators understand the subtleties of marketing language, so your sales message is never lost in translation.

With the skills and professionalism of a large agency, we also give you the personal attention that only a small, local company can provide.

You can see for yourself. Just let me know and I'll email across a few recent examples of our work along with client testimonials. Or, if you have a moment, I could call in any time and show you myself.

You can email me at vlatka@poleposition.com or call me on 06789 7654321.

Thank you,

Vlatka Komorowski

(Manager, Pole Position)

FACEBOOK

**Disseminate information and be
more than just 'liked'**

If LinkedIn is a gigantic networking event for businesses, Facebook is the cool club across town where you can hang out with all the customers.

Don't get any ideas about barging in, setting up stall and selling your wares, however.

Facebook is all about making friends – the sales come later.

WHAT'S IN THIS CHAPTER?

❶ YOUR NON-BUSINESS PLAN

Facebook is a place where relationships are built and reputations are made by being a part of the community.

By focusing on the social side of your business, you can bond with users in a more enduring and financially rewarding way than by making a clumsy attempt at short-term sales.

Be social

Just by being on Facebook, you are putting yourself where your customers are.

Whether your objective is to...

  O Boost awareness of your products and services

  O Gather feedback from your target market

  O Raise awareness of your company website

...Facebook marketing is really about two things:

1 Lots of people getting to know your business

2 Your business getting to know lots of people

Facebook provides this social arena for free (you can pay for advertisements, but that's not what we are bothered about here). It also includes a range of free features to make getting to know your community easy. 'Insights', for example, provides in-depth statistics about who is showing interest in you, and you can create and join Groups for people with shared interests.

Become a Facebook sensation

Here's how it works...

Create a personal timeline

Your timeline is a personal space where you can interact and share photographs, videos, news and anything else with the Facebook community.

↓

Make friends

Friends are people you connect and share stuff with.

↓

Create a business page

Your business page is a space where your business can interact and share photographs, videos, news and anything else with the Facebook community.

↓

Post interesting things

A post is a comment, or other media, that you place on your page to stimulate a response (rather than simply be seen).

↓

Be shared

Users can post or share a page with whoever they wish.

↓

Be liked

When someone clicks 'Like' on your post, it is noted under the item, on their timeline and possibly in their news feed. When someone likes your page, they can receive updates from it in their news feed.

↓

Appear in news feeds

A news feed is a continually updated list on a user's homepage that details their friends' activities, such as pages they have liked.

↓

Become a Facebook sensation

People see in their news feed that their friends have liked your page. They visit your page. They like it too.

...and interest in your page continues to increase until Facebook is abuzz with your business.

People see in their news feed that their friends have liked your page.

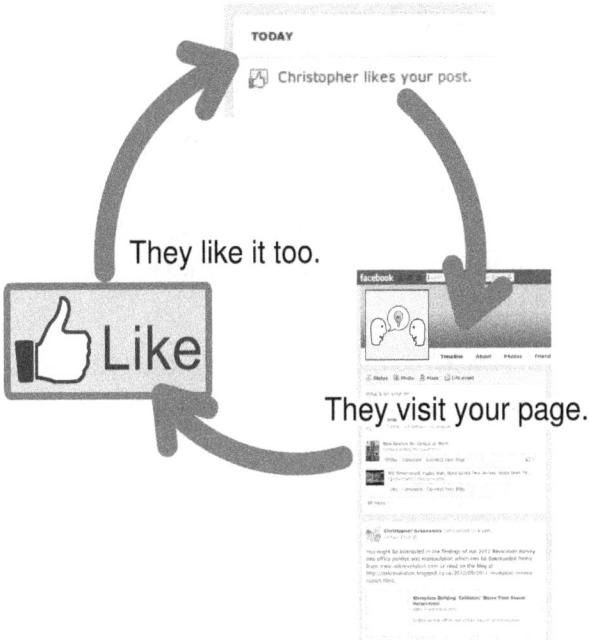

They like it too.

They visit your page.

Become a Facebook sensation

If your posts are not up to scratch, however, the outcome is not so good:

↓

Become a Facebook failure

Your posts are dull. Nothing gets liked. Your business page sits unnoticed, like an ancient tin of Cannellini beans gathering dust at the back of the cupboard.

The key to Facebook success
Create likeable, shareable, interactive posts that will resound around your target community.

Spread the word

Posting content is not the only thing you can do to drum up interest in your business page.

You can…

- ❍ Put your Facebook username on everything. Online, this means using a clickable link at the foot of your blog post or website. Offline, it means adding your username to all your stationary and promotional material.

- ❍ Interact with other pages by answering questions and offering advice, while leaving a link back to your own page.

- ❍ Get involved with groups that share common interests.

- ❍ Invite friends from your personal account to visit and like your business page.

- ❍ Email people connected to your business, including suppliers and customers. Suggest they check out your Facebook page and like it to receive updates in their own news feeds.

- ❍ Use Facebook Ads to promote your page. These are targeted pay-per-click advertisements that appear in the margins of other users' timelines.

❷ SET-UP

Unlike most marketing opportunities, Facebook favours cash-strapped independents over the moneyed corporation.

The personal nature of Facebook means that slick professionalism would simply be out of place. Fortunately for us, Facebook's house style is unsophisticated and amateurish.

Your personal timeline

Before you can achieve anything with your business on Facebook, you need to have a personal account. Once you are registered, you will be able to create your personal profile, or timeline as Facebook calls it.

A timeline is like your own website within the Facebook world. Unlike a website, however, it is not a snapshot of your present-day situation, it is a scroll through time, showing whatever you have chosen to share in chronological order. It can incorporate such things as your contact details, relationships, work and education as well as everything from your favourite colour to your thoughts on the trend towards secularisation in the western world.

» Be personal (with business in mind)

Remember, your timeline is not about your business. It is just about you and it provides a way for people to get to know you. Take the opportunity to throw off your business mask for a minute and let your genuine personality come to the fore.

Having said that, the people that view your timeline may also be potential customers. So, posting about the drunken night you covered the local scout hut in lewd graffiti, isn't going to make a favourable impression.

Your business page

Once your personal account is in place, you can create a business page. Of course, if you are a small-scale sole trader you may wish to stick with just your personal timeline, though a business page presents more of an opportunity to sell yourself.

A business page has a timeline similar to your personal profile. Here is some advice on its basic content.

» Profile picture

For a sole-trader, the mugshot that accompanies your page (called an Avatar by people that like to pretend they are in a sci-fi film) should just be a straightforward picture of your smiling face. Alternatively, you may want to use an attractive image that represents your field of work.

Whatever you choose, it is worth spending time to equip yourself with an image that is clear, sharp and interesting (i.e. not an impersonal company logo).

A supplier of pottery from around the world uses an attractive ethnic vase as its profile picture.

What Facebook users want
People don't go to Facebook to read, they go for friendly fun and interesting insight – and your profile picture is your first chance to give it to them.

» Cover photo

This is a large image that sits at the top of your timeline. Instead of going for a picture of your favourite football team or a basket of kittens, choose something striking that is relevant to you and your brand. An eye-catching picture of your star product, for example. If you are a creative business, you may want to use your cover photo to showcase your work.

A photographer uses his cover photo like a portfolio, displaying a different image every week.

» Information

When describing your business, keep it short and to the point. You can include more details elsewhere. Remember to add your full contact information so that people aren't restricted to contacting you by your Facebook page alone. Include keywords where possible. These will be picked up by people searching for anything in your field.

A company hosting corporate team-building events mentions all their past clients by name so that anyone searching for their clients will also find them.

» Applications

You can add extra functionality to your page by taking advantage of a range of applications, such as embedded YouTube videos or an RSS feed direct from your blog.

» URL

The initial URL of your business page consists predominantly of numbers:

```
www.facebook.com/pages/MyBusiness/372964033982
```

Something like that is not going to look very nice on your business card and letterhead. However, once your page is established, you are able to change this for a much nicer one:

```
www.facebook.com/pages/MyBusiness
```

This customer-friendly address is also your Facebook username.

❸ POSTS

Your business page isn't an online newsletter, pronouncing to a passive public, it is your very own public playground.

Provide a creative and stimulating page, and people will come to explore, join in and have fun – and they'll invite their friends along too. With a ready supply of imaginative, interactive posts, your page will be as popular as Alton Towers on a Bank Holiday Monday.

What makes a successful post?

Successful posts turn your page into a dynamic, interactive hub of interesting things to see, comment on and (most importantly) share with others. So, before you decide what to post, you need to know what kind of post will resonate with your community.

» Give them what they want

Think visually and think short. Research into Facebook shows that the items that people share the most are photographs, videos and questions. And whenever words are involved, people are much, much more likely to share it if it is shorter than 50 words.

» Bolster your brand

Your posts help to form an opinion in people's minds, so make sure it is a favourable one. Show the personality of your brand, be approachable and, at all times, be professional ('friendly' professional, not formal).

» Encourage interaction

Think of your posts as a two-way conversation, not a statement. Posts that consist of nothing more than a link to something else, for example, will go largely unnoticed, because they do not draw the reader into a dialogue.

» Post regularly

Maintain the conversation. If you unilaterally discontinue the communication with your Facebook community, they won't hang around for your posts to spring back to life. It doesn't matter whether you post daily, weekly or monthly, just be consistent. It will only take around 10 minutes each time.

If your don't have 10 minutes to spare, you can schedule posts to be uploaded onto Facebook at a future date. You could do a week's worth of daily posts each weekend, for example, then add any topical ones as they occur. If you schedule your posts, you should still check your page daily to reply to any comments left in response.

Getting into news feeds

Most Facebook users are connected to lots of pages and groups, which would make their news feed an unmanageable torrent, were it not for EdgeRank.

EdgeRank is an algorithm used by Facebook to ensure users receive only the most desirable content for news feeds. I won't bore you with how it does it, suffice it to say, your posts will get in more of other people's news feeds if they are:

- New - Fresh content always trumps previous content from weeks gone by.

- Popular - Receiving likes, comments and shares from lots of different people.

- Consistent - Receiving regular likes, comments and shares from the same people.

What to put in your posts

Choosing what to put in your posts so that people will interact with them, like, share and comment on them, is like a teenager choosing clothes to wear to an all-important party. Even if you get it right, show any hint of over-thinking it or making a self-consciousness attempt at being cool, and you will be exposed as an uncool fraud. It needs to be carried out with natural, effortless ease.

> *Rule #1: Have fun*
> What will people find fun about what your business does? Express that in all your Facebook content.

Here's how to pull it off in a way that makes your business seem cooler than Fonzie eating an ice cream on the North Pole.

» Pictures

When you have something to say, say it visually if possible. Well targeted images have instant impact and are eminently shareable.

Every month, a retailer of contemporary jewellery, uploads a picture of that month's birthstone. This is soon shared by hundreds of interested followers with anyone having a birthday that month.

» Image tags

If your image has someone in it, tag them. A tag is a link that connects the post with that person's timeline. Tagging an image helps it spread faster and further.

A vinyl record shop organises a band to play at their premises. They upload photographs of the audience to Facebook and ask them to tag themselves. Each tag appears in the user's news feed, which spreads news of the event, and the record shop, to all their friends.

» Words on your picture

When you have something to say, but can't say it visually, put the words onto a picture.

Wetta, a manufacturer of refreshing juice drinks, posts a 'Where's Wally' type of image showing a hot summer's day at the seaside. A carton of their juice is hidden somewhere in the picture. Text overlaid along the top of the image says:

Where's Wetta? Free pack for the first 100 people to spot the Wetta carton.

Or, it could be a simple question.

> An independent fashion retailer invited opinion by posting an image of three party dresses along with the question, 'Snog, marry or avoid?'. People responded with what they thought and shared the image with their friends.

» Videos

A clip of something striking, interesting or helpful will garner far more attention than one showing the managing director giving a lacklustre 'welcome' spiel.

> A restaurant aimed at the youthful end of the market posts a short video of its chef performing his party piece, where he puts one hand on a chopping board and proceeds to stab the spaces between his fingers with a kitchen knife at an alarming speed.

Use your video to gather a crowd by encouraging a response.

> A company organising cycling holidays, posts regular bicycle repair 'how to' videos and uses them to stimulate conversations about the wider topic of cycling, thus tapping into the cycling community.

» Questions

The best way to begin a conversation is with a question, preferably one that requires only a short, simple answer.

> A financial advisor asks: "Renting is better than home ownership - Yes or No?"

'Fill in the blank' questions written in the first person ('I' instead of 'you' or 'he/her') are a good way to catch the eye of people skimming through their news feed.

A recruitment company posts: "If I could have any job in the world, it would be ___."

Treat your viewers like experts in your field of work by asking their advice. It's a great way to collect valuable feedback.

A speciality beer retailer asks: "Can you suggest a beer that we should stock?"

Once a conversation starts, don't ignore it. Answer any questions left for you, especially if they are in any way critical of your business.

» News

Keep your page regularly updated with daily news about your business. No, I don't mean the release of the quarterly sales estimates, I mean something that:

1 Is actually happening

2 Will make Facebook users feel privileged

3 People might want to share or comment on

For example:

- Revealing new products on Facebook

- Something that an industry bigwig has just said

- An upcoming event

To which you could follow up afterwards with:

- Announcing when the new product is available

- Comments that start a debate on the subject

- Exclusive photos from the event

» Topical comments

Your Facebook page may be for your business, but you are posting to catch the interest of real people – people that don't spend every waking hour thinking about your business.

These people will be more likely to notice your page if you include topics that reach out beyond the obvious boundaries of your business.

A sports club asks:

> **Church Street Sports Club**
> Who will win the FA Cup Final?
> Like · Comment · Share · 3 hours ago ·

Comment on what interests them, not you

Your remarks do not have to have any relation at all to your business.

A Public Relations company posts...

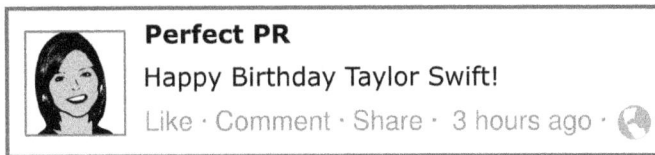

> **Perfect PR**
> Happy Birthday Taylor Swift!
> Like · Comment · Share · 3 hours ago ·

...knowing it will catch a lot of people's attention.

What with breaking news, the weather, celebrity gossip and the fact that virtually every day of the year is 'something-or-other day', there is no shortage of topical things to comment on.

» Inside information

Providing tasty morsels of inside information will soon have people coming back for more. For example, people always like to hear someone else spill the beans. So any behind the scenes gossip or privileged access is sure to attract interest.

An IT company posts their own photographs and comments from a visit to CeBIT, the world's largest high-tech event.

Or why not share your expertise? Free advice will attract a loyal following among potential users of your service.

A plumbing company posts tips on preventing pipes freezing in winter:

Perfect Plumbing
Why frozen water will burst your pipes

1 Water expands by 9% when it freezes

2 Cold air makes unprotected pipes freeze

3 Water pressure caused by the blocked pipe causes the pipe to split at a weak point

4 When the temperature rises and the pipe thaws, water leaks out

Like · Comment · Share · 3 hours ago ·

» Responses

Facebook interaction is a two-way process, so a large proportion of your posts should be generated by responding to others' posts. Take time to read comments on your page and encourage a conversation with those that leave them, regardless of whether they are favourable or not. The quicker you respond to questions and criticism, the more loyalty you will build amongst your following. So don't delay.

> *Don't broadcast – have conversations*
> Imagine you are sat around a table with your Facebook friends. Talk with them, not at them.

One way to make responding fast and easy is to use your mobile phone. You can download a Facebook app for smart phones that alerts you whenever someone interacts in some way with your page. This allows you to jump on negative comments and respond to them immediately.

And remember, it's not all about you – so feel free to socialise and comment on other people's and business's pages, like their posts and generally get yourself out and about in your Facebook neighbourhood.

» Freebies

Describe a service or product you don't mind giving away, preferably with a great picture. Then offer it as an incentive to get people spreading your message.

A food takeaway business posts:

Priceless Pizza
Each time you share this photo of our new Mega Meaty Pizza, you will be entered into a draw to win a FREE one.

Like · Comment · Share · 3 hours ago ·

Incentives can also be used to encourage customers to promote your business via their personal posts.

A hairdresser takes before and after pictures of their customers then offers discount haircuts for those that post them online.

» Events

Instigate an event and encourage everyone involved to spread the word on Facebook. The choice of possible events is limitless.

It could be online:

A garden centre holds a monthly webinar to help with gardening problems. Users' interaction with the event will appear in their news feeds.

It could be offline:

An IT consultant promotes a demonstration he is giving on the latest office technology, and states that full details of the event are available on his Facebook page.

It could be made up:

An architects holds a 'Love your home' day where people can show their bricks and mortar how much they are appreciated. They ask people to post photographs on their page showing themselves patting their walls etc.

» Call to action

Once you have built up a significant level of engagement with your page, you can harness that interest with a call to action of some sort. This doesn't mean commanding followers to Buy Now! Rather, it needs to incorporate an inducement to respond to your posts in a particular way.

For example, you may wish people to...

Click on a link:

A cookery school posts a link to a delicious recipe – that is located on their website, along with details of their courses.

Share a post:

A car valeting company posts a '20% off' voucher on Valentines Day overlaid with the words "I LOVE YOUr car", and suggests you send it to the car lover in your life.

Comment on what you have said:

A handyman asks people to tell him of a DIY job that they've been meaning to do in their home, but never got around to it. He says that at the end of the week he'll put them all into a hat, pick one out and do it for free. In the meantime, he has gathered a pile of potential clients in need of a handyman.

FLYERS

**Spread the word with hand-outs
people hang on to**

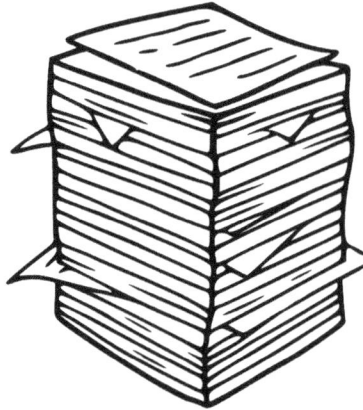

Whether it is being used to promote a product, a service, a sale or an event, the sheer simplicity and tactile nature of a flyer make it less ignorable and more likely to be read than most other forms of marketing communication.

Packing a huge amount of promotional clout in just a few words and a physical form that fits in a back pocket, the flyer is the Tardis of the marketing universe.

What's in this Chapter?

❶ THE FOCUSED FLYER

Flyers are relatively quick and cheap to produce and distribute, which is why there are so many of them about. However, many flyers simply crash land into the nearest bin. Either their offer is too complex to engage readers' attention or they are written without any understanding of the customer, meaning they will miss their target completely.

By making one simple offer to one clearly identified market, your flyer will cut through the promotional ether like a customer-seeking missile.

One offer

When deciding what message to convey on their flyer, many business owners find it hard to contain themselves. They want to say everything. As a result, they say virtually nothing at all.

To prevent your flyer having all the firmness of purpose of a blancmange, think of it like a trailer for a film: a concise, powerful piece of promotion to whet the appetite of the audience, with every word and image focusing on a single, unambiguous offer.

> *Give your flyer a clear focus. Either:*
> 1. A solution to the reader's problem
> 2. Something to the reader wants

'A solution to the reader's problem' includes such remedies as *stop roofs leaking, cut costs, gain peace of mind* or *improve fitness.*

'Something the reader wants' includes such aspirations as *less time doing housework, exclusive luxury chocolates, a faster PC* or *a cheap holiday.*

If your flyer loses its focus at any point or, worse still, has no focus at all other than to say 'we are here', the reader will immediately lose interest.

Ali Barber, a local barbershop, provides the usual hair-cutting service for a wide range of clientèle. However, for their promotional flyer, they decide to focus on a single issue: encouraging parents to bring their children in for a 'back to school' haircut at the end of the school summer break.

One market

Who your prospective customers are dictates everything from what you put on your flyer to where and how you choose to distribute it.

> *Tailor your flyer to a specific market*
> Understand the people who will be receiving your flyer – and what will make them act on your offer.

It would be great if you could tailor each flyer to suit each individual that receives it, but that would defeat the mass-distribution objective of the flyer (if you want something more one-to-one, see the Sales Letter chapter of this book). Instead, it is possible to group people together according to their shared characteristics. That might be their job, their age, where they live, the fact that they have just dropped young children off at nursery... whatever identifies the kind of people that would benefit from your flyer's offer.

There may be more than one distinct market, in which case it is better to print, say, three lots of 500 precision-targeted flyers rather than 1,500 non-specific ones.

A local beauty parlour offering all kinds of treatments decides to target a flyer towards middle-aged women. They understand the concerns of this group, and focus the flyer on the kind of treatments that would appeal to this particular market. Another flyer of theirs targets younger women, focusing solely on the kind of treatments that appeal to that age group.

Ali Barber's flyers are targeted at parents of school-age children, particularly primary school age.

❷ ESSENTIALS

A flyer dominated by the business's logo, a picture of the business's premises and a photo of the business owner's smiling face might make the business owner happy, but it's not what potential customers are interested in.

Readers need a reason to take action and, like a BLT sandwich, a successful flyer has three irresistible ingredients that, when taken in together, leave people wanting more:

1. A compelling headline

2. Clear benefits

3. An incentive to act.

Headline

Once you have clarified an unambiguous recipient for your unambiguous offer, you need to convey your offer in an unambiguous headline.

The headline should dominate your flyer so that the recipients' eyes land on it immediately. The wording should strike right at the heart of readers' concerns, so they are unable to ignore it. It should evoke the improvements it will make to their life and stir an enthusiasm that will encourage them to read on.

Here's how you go about it.

» Address needs

For your headline to connect with the person reading it, it must be about something that concerns them.

A nail salon's flyer would go largely unnoticed with the headline:

Nail Salon

But it would strike a chord with its target customers by addressing their needs with the pertinent question:

Are your nails letting you down?

» Evoke benefits

Say what difference the product or service will make to readers' lives.

A photographer's flyer would fail to interest its readers with the lifeless headline:

Photography

But they would respond to a headline that arouses a feeling of the benefit that could be enjoyed:

Memories that never fade

» Excite interest

To word your headline in such a way that will hook in customers, you need to entice them with the benefit rather than try to tell the whole story.

A pizza take-away's flyer would fail to excite any interest with the headline:

Pizza Take-Away

But any parent would be intrigued enough to look further with this headline:

Feed the family tonight for only £10

Ali Barber uses a two-pronged, tongue-in-cheek headline that will make any parent of school-age children look twice:

BACK TO SCHOOL

Don't let bad hair hold your child back!

Benefits

When you've marched the reader up to the top of the hill with a rousing headline, it isn't the time to bore them rigid with the equivalent of your website's About Us page. Neither should you reward their interest with an inadequate follow-up that would leave them feeling short-changed.

You need to maintain the level of interest you provoked with the headline while moving them on by answering their fundamental question: "What's in it for me?"

» Less is more

The trick to knowing what to say, is knowing what not to say. Even the most likely prospect does not want to know all about it at this stage. You could hand them an encyclopedic guidebook on the thing and make them sit through a PowerPoint presentation about it, and they would remain unmoved.

The flyer does not tell the reader everything, it prompts them to investigate further. At this stage, all potential customers want to know – in as few words as possible – is how you can help them.

» Offer solutions to problems

People are motivated by their needs. So, ask yourself what it is that your prospective customers really need that you can help them with?

- People don't worry because they want a personal trainer, they worry because they can't lose weight.

- People don't worry because they want to learn Spanish, they worry because they are unable to order food and ask directions when on holiday in Spain.

Then, you can either raise one or two questions that empathise with their concerns (which will make your offer of a solution all the more welcome)...

Have you tried everything under the sun to lose weight?

Or you can give three or four punchy, benefit-led points stating how you can remedy their concerns.

Don't be lost for words when you go abroad this summer

Ali Barber's flyer provides the following solutions to parents' needs:

Boys and girls welcome

This is unusual and saves parents with young girls and boys the hassle of dragging them all along to two different places for a haircut.

Every hairstyle possible

Reassures parents and fussy kids wanting something specific that they can get it here.

We like kids – even the ones who don't like haircuts

Cutting toddlers' hair can be a nightmare, and many hairdressers are not good at dealing with it, causing stress and embarrassment for the parent.

The eye must fall naturally on these benefits after the initial hook of the headline, so don't hide them away.

Then you need to move the eye swiftly on again without losing momentum.

Incentive

Although the flyer lies somewhere in-between the publicity seeking advertisement and the information providing leaflet, its role is more straightforward than either of them. It is a prompt to act. It publicises and informs just enough to provoke a positive response from the reader.

Think of it as the difference between courting the apple of your eye with flowers, chocolates, romantic meals... and speed dating. A flyer is saying: "Here I am. Yes or no?" It may not be romantic, but it gets the job done.

The headline and benefits provide the 'Here I am' bit. Now you need to pull out all the stops to maximise your chances of getting a 'Yes'. It just takes one lull in the positive vibe for all your good work to be rendered null and void. So, how do you ensure a positive initial impression leads to a positive response?

» Clubs, carrots & coupons

Providing all the ways the reader can get in touch with you (phone numbers, address, website address, email) does not give them a reason to call now. Even adding the instruction to 'Call Now' does not give the reader a reason to call now. What is required is an incentive to act.

Your incentive may take the form of:

- A club, hitting readers with the bad things that will happen if they don't respond now.

- A carrot, offering readers something worthwhile if they respond, such as the very flyer-friendly coupon.

Whatever you choose, don't hide it away in the small print, make it unmissable alongside your contact details. Of course, if your incentive is especially attractive – it should be in the headline.

Example clubs...

Don't risk waiting until winter to have your boiler serviced

Warnings like this bring a genuine concern to the forefront of the reader's mind.

Can you afford not to use a business coach?

This kind of phrase prompts the reader to imagine the negative consequences of disregarding the offer.

Example carrots...

Buy before {date} and get {discount} off

This has the benefit of inducing immediate action, but the downside of cutting into your profits. An alternative is to offer something less costly to you, such as a free CD or a free report.

To cut your energy bills by 20% call us on...

This simply reminds the reader what the flyer is all about. It implies that they have nothing to lose but plenty to gain.

Example coupons...

Coupons are a way to give your prospects a benefit they can feel in their hands immediately. They are also a good way to measure the success of your campaign. There are three types of coupon:

1   The free sample coupon

Offering your prospect the chance to send a coupon to you in return for a free gift of some sort is a way to give them a taste of your products, and provide you with valuable contact information.

2 The redemption coupon

Offering something in exchange for the coupon, such as a free coffee at a new café, for example, is a way to get the customer into your premises, where they will be exposed to further buying opportunities.

3 The discount coupon

Offering something off the cost of your products or services, and giving the holder the freedom to choose what they use it on, is a great way to introduce people to what you can do for them.

Whichever type of coupon is suitable for your flyer, make sure it:

- *O* Is clear and simple to understand

- *O* Prominently displays a clear benefit (e.g. 'Save £5')

- *O* Has an expiration date on it

Ali Barber provides a coupon designed to encourage customers to make the effort to visit his barbershop:

GET

£2 OFF

ANY CHILD'S HAIRCUT AT

Ali Barber

Visit us before the end of the summer hols and get £2 off any child's haircut with this coupon.
Offer available until Saturday 2nd September.

---

③ EXTRAS

While the essentials just described should take centre stage, there is room on your flyer for a few extras to play a supporting role.

Images

Your flyer is focused on making an offer in a way that addresses the reader's self-interest. The same message can be conveyed visually too, so that the words and pictures work in harmony. Here are some tips for using images on your flyer...

- *Ø* Make sure they are relevant and meaningful (rather than nice-looking but gratuitous)

- *Ø* Consider the page as a whole rather than imposing artificial newspaper-like boundaries on where words and images must go

- *Ø* One large image has more impact than a number of smaller ones

- *Ø* Don't allow images to detract from the text

- *Ø* Depending on you product or service, before-and-after pictures are a good way to demonstrate benefits

Use good quality photography that will impress the reader. If it is a product you are selling, you may well have good quality photographs already. If it is a service, such as financial advice or training, you may want to choose something from one of the many online photo-libraries. Whatever you do, avoid using clip art images. They look cheap and give the reader the impression they are dealing with a schoolchild rather than a serious business.

Ali Barber uses an appropriate illustration to emphasise the message conveyed in his flyer:

Pass it on

For no additional cost and no detriment to the overall message, it is possible to circumvent the instinctive jettisoning of the unwanted flyer by encouraging the recipient to 'Pass it on'.

Place a short piece of text at the bottom of the front page, maybe in the bottom corner, saying something like:

> Know someone who could use this offer? Pass it on!

Or:

> Not interested? Pass me on to someone who is.

Not everyone will be moved by this request. However, there will be some who read it and immediately recall someone they know who is looking for whatever you are offering. Then, when the flyer is passed on it comes with the added kudos of a personal referral, which dramatically increases your flyer's chance of success.

The other front side

The reverse side of your flyer has almost as much value as the front. In fact, for many people taking a look at your flyer, it will be the first side they see. Use the flip side wisely and you double the flyer's promotional power.

Keep your eye-catching marketing message (headline, benefits and incentive) together on the front. Then put supporting information on the back. Think of the front as Batman and the back as Robin. Together they are unstoppable.

The supporting information on the back of your flyer could include such things as:

- A map
- A menu
- A price list
- Before and after photos
- Professional qualifications
- Relevant news clippings
- FAQs
- Testimonials

There is an exception to using the reverse side of your flyer. If it is intended to be pinned to noticeboards or pasted on walls, then, of course, leave the back blank.

On the reverse of the Ali Barber flyer are fun testimonials from kids that provide reassurance for parents considering bringing their own children in for a haircut.

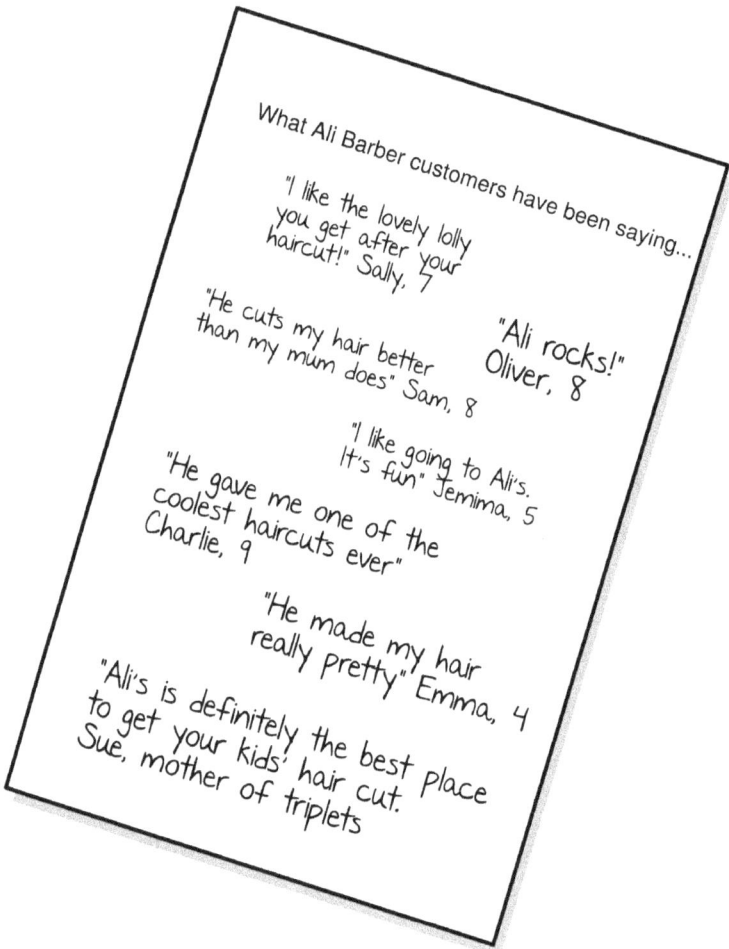

What Ali Barber customers have been saying...

"I like the lovely lolly you get after your haircut!" Sally, 7

"He cuts my hair better than my mum does" Sam, 8

"Ali rocks!" Oliver, 8

"I like going to Ali's. It's fun" Jemima, 5

"He gave me one of the coolest haircuts ever" Charlie, 9

"He made my hair really pretty" Emma, 4

"Ali's is definitely the best place to get your kids' hair cut. Sue, mother of triplets

❹ IMPACT

You have created the content for your flyer. Now you need to do what you can to increase the chances of a successful campaign. So, before anyone sets out with a stack of flyers under your arm, before you even pass it to the printer, read this.

Design

The recipient doesn't want to expend any effort whatsoever when they receive your flyer, so a simple, instantly comprehensible message is more likely to be pocketed, pinned on a noticeboard or attached to the fridge door than one that requires some level of deciphering.

While each individual element may be as unmissable as a blast from a trumpet, bringing your headline, benefits, incentive and imagery together can easily result in a cacophonous mishmash. Here are some tips on ensuring your message doesn't get lost in the design.

» Branding

Business owners love to see their branding become the centre of attention. Logo, company name, slogan, graphics, typeface... the bigger and more prominent the better. However, it is not the business owner the flyer is intended to please, it is the prospective customer. Expressing the offer to the reader is paramount, and this must take precedence over the branding.

Put another way: flyers don't give you much space to play with – so the smaller your logo, the more room you have to present your offer to the reader.

» Font

Don't try to impress the reader with numerous fonts and formatting styles. The clarity of your message is all that is important, so choose a font that is easy to read with a quick glance and large enough to be read without the need for glasses.

» Colours

As with fonts, numerous colours will not improve the chances of your flyer's success, though using contrasting colours can bolster the appearance of the message. Clarity is what it is all about, so avoid trying to get noticed by using garish colours as they are irrelevant to what you are saying (unless you are promoting a rave event).

» Images

See the comments made earlier about imagery – especially the bit about not using clip art. As well as online photo libraries there are a host of free resources (which can soon be accessed with a little help from Google) where you can find powerful, relevant images.

» Paper

The size and thickness of your flyer should suit your target audience. If, for example, you are distributing flyers through letterboxes, you want something robust enough (say, 300gsm) to survive being posted and last long enough until the recipient requires your services. If, on the other hand, you are handing out flyers on a busy street to tell people of a 'Free coffee today with this flyer', then something lighter (say, 150gsm) and pocket-sized (say, A6) would be fine.

A poorly designed flyer gives a poor impression of your business. People will not have any qualms about discarding a flyer with all the style and grace of a piece of toilet paper, but they might think twice about throwing away a flyer with a stunning image and an attractive message printed on high-quality paper.

It is worthwhile assembling the flyer's content yourself, then handing it to a professional designer to put together. Before hiring a designer, take a look at their portfolio. When you have decided who to use, you will be able to send them your content electronically.

Distribution

The recipients of your flyer should be as well-defined as possible to maximise its effective distribution.

For example...

- ✪ Luxury car valet service - Put flyers under the wipers of luxury cars
- ✪ Kids clothing - Hand flyers to parents dropping kids off at a nursery
- ✪ A sandwich shop - Deliver to local businesses
- ✪ A marketing consultant - Hand out to visitors at a SME conference
- ✪ Music event promotions - Distribute as people leave music venues

As with advertisements in magazines or on television, one outing for a flyer is seldom enough to reach all potential customers. Flyers can be re-distributed two or three times at least. And, while you are at it, they can be pinned on local information boards, in the newsagent's window, on the notice board in the dentist's waiting room, wherever will catch the eyes of your target reader.

Ali Barber, targeting parents of school-age children, leaves flyers in the kids' section of the local libraries, local grocery stores, newsagents, the Post Office, as well as distributing them to homes in family residential areas.

Ali Barber

49 Main Street, Coppleton

BACK TO SCHOOL

DON'T LET BAD HAIR HOLD YOUR CHILD BACK!

Ali Barber specialises in smart haircuts for smart kids...

- ✂ Boys _and_ girls welcome
- ✂ Every hairstyle possible
- ✂ We like kids – even the ones that don't like haircuts

Visit Ali Barber 9am-5pm Tuesday-Saturday
49 Main Street, Coppleton 01234 123123
No appointment necessary

GET **£2 OFF** ANY CHILD'S HAIRCUT AT Ali Barber

Visit us before the end of the summer hols and get £2 off any child's haircut with this coupon. Offer available until Saturday 2nd September.

(Not interested? Please pass it on to someone who is.)

er customers have been saying...

lovely lolly
after your
Sally, 7

"Ali rocks!" Oliver, 8

hair better
n does" Sam, 8

"I like going to Ali's. It's fun" Jemima, 5

ie one of the
rcuts ever"

"He made my hair really pretty" Emma, 4

finitely the best place to get your kids' hair cut. Sue, mother of triplets

Ali Barber flyer – front and back

LINKEDIN

**Get noticed in the world's largest
business-based social media**

LinkedIn may be a social media platform, but personal interaction is strictly business.

You don't chat with friends – you have exchanges with business contacts. You don't organise parties – you leverage your professional network (whatever that means).

This may make LinkedIn seem as much fun as an Excel spreadsheet, but if you want to build a business's brand and cultivate business relationships, LinkedIn is, er, the business.

What's in this Chapter?

❶ NETWORKING ON STEROIDS

Networking is the invisible force that brings all the elements of a growing enterprise together. Whether a business is in need of customers, suppliers, investors, new employees or background information on another business, the solution can typically be found among their network of contacts.

While traditional networking involves exchanging business cards with a couple of colleagues over a sausage roll and a glass of wine, LinkedIn is a supercharged system that allows businesses to network better, further and faster than ever before possible.

Build the ultimate business network

There is a concept known as six degrees of separation that describes how everyone is no more than six connections away from anyone else in the world. Mick Jagger and I, for example, are practically brothers: my milkman went on holiday to Florida where he befriended a lady whose brother works for a woman who is married to a guy that used to roadie for the Rolling Stones.

LinkedIn works in the same way. You build up a network of connections, which gives you a secondary connection to your connections' connections and so on.

Your personal network is defined as everyone within three degrees of separation and, when you carry out a search within LinkedIn, results are prioritised according to your network proximity.

Amy is a yoga teacher who has LinkedIn connections with most of her regular clients.

Dave is a freelance financial consultant on the other side of town who wants to learn yoga – so he enters 'yoga teacher' into LinkedIn's search box. The results Dave sees are prioritised according to their closeness within his personal network.

Dave has a connection to Charles, the owner of a second-hand bookshop (he uses Dave's financial services). Charles has a connection to Bill, a web designer (he created a website for Charles's bookshop). Bill attends Amy's yoga class, and is connected to her on LinkedIn.

So, when Dave searches for 'yoga teacher', Amy's name will appear at the top of the list (unless there is another yoga teacher within fewer degrees of separation). Dave may either contact Amy himself, by looking up her details, or pass a message to her via Charles and Bill.

Amy   Bill   Charles   Dave

3 degrees of separation

Contacts found within a LinkedIn personal network are...

» Meaningful

In contrast to other social media sites, where connections are made with any Tom, Dick or Harriette, LinkedIn connections are made with known and trusted business associates.

» Abundant

There are over 225 million LinkedIn members, any of whom you can find out more about and communicate with.

» Accessible

Simply send a LinkedIn invite to an associate asking if they will join your network. When an invitation is accepted, both the inviter and the invitee are automatically added to each other's network.

When you have maximised the number of personal connections and pushed your network to the limit, carefully crafted LinkedIn pages can draw in potential clients and key individuals from far and wide – which is what the rest of this chapter is about.

Out-Google Google

Wait a minute, you may be thinking. Why bother with all of this LinkedIn malarkey when we already have the world wide web and Google, the greatest (allegedly) method of finding and being found in the world?

Well, let's compare the two methods...

A bigwig in a big business is desperate to award a big contract to someone who can supply precisely what Bob's business is the bees knees at supplying.

With Google, identifying Bob as the ideal supplier is like trying to find a needle in a world wide haystack.

With LinkedIn, it is like finding a needle in a neat collection of needles that:

- ✔ have been categorised according to location and numerous other attributes
- ✔ have their individual capabilities and specialisms clearly on display
- ✔ come with a set of recommendations from respected members of the local Sewing Circle.

Not surprisingly, therefore, LinkedIn is very popular with businesses and individuals that want to find others and be found themselves.

❷ GETTING NOTICED

Getting a business or individual established on LinkedIn initially involves filling in personal details – skills, education, that sort of thing. This is great for impressing the people that visit the page, but here we are going to look at writing the content that will attract them to the page in the first place.

Personal profile

Once an account has been created, LinkedIn will ask you to set up a personal profile. This is an opportunity to sell the individual, not their business. You can include all kinds of things in a personal profile, but it is the headline and summary that really get a person noticed by other LinkedIn members.

> *The primary objective is to be found*
> Your personal profile is not for you, it's for your target audience – so they can discover you and be impressed by what they read.

Headline

Your headline is the only bit of your personal information that will be visible in search results – apart from your name and location, which you can't exactly customise. It is entirely down to your headline, therefore, to lure the right people in so they can check out your profile in full.

Sarah James' business, Grapheek, expresses complicated technical information using clear, simple visual techniques. Her default headline is uninspiring and of limited use:

```
Sarah James
Grapheek
```

To transform this piece of wasted space into something more meaningful and worthwhile, you need to use your headline to state your marketing message.

You have 120 characters to play with, so make the most of them to produce a sales pitch that will resonate with the people you want to find you on LinkedIn.

» How to create a 'marketing message' headline

To develop an effective profile headline, you need to assemble information about your market, what they are looking for and what you have to offer them.

This may seem like a lot of effort for such a small piece of text, but it isn't. Just think of it like a quick survey. So let's get started with the first question…

Question 1: who will be searching for you?

It may not be the person that will use your services at this stage. Clarify who it is and target your message towards them.

Question 2: what search terms will they use?

Whatever they are, these are your keywords. Try to include these key keywords twice in your headline.

Question 3: what will they get out of hiring you?

State the benefits your products or service will bring to the prospective client.

> ## Question 4: what extra qualities do you have to offer?
>
> This may include technical qualifications, or adjectives that help you stand out from the competition.
>
> ## Question 5: is there any creative flair you can add to your job description?
>
> A bit of wit and charm can help a headline get noticed.

Collate your answers, string them together in a logical order, then trim to fit – and you have a headline that tells the reader with succinct vigour precisely what is in it for them.

Here's how Sarah James from Grapheek followed this process to improve her headline...

> ## Question 1: who will be searching for you?
>
> Managers in the IT/technology industry
>
> ## Question 2: what search terms will they use?
>
> Graphic Design, Technical, IT
>
> ## Question 3: what will they get out of hiring you?
>
> Innovative graphic design for technical communications
>
> ## Question 4: what extra qualities do you have to offer?
>
> Technical literacy
>
> ## Question 5: can you add a dash of creativity to your job description?
>
> The company name reflects a love of technology and graphics: Geek + Graphic = Grapheek!

This information is used to create a 'marketing message' headline for Sarah James that says it all:

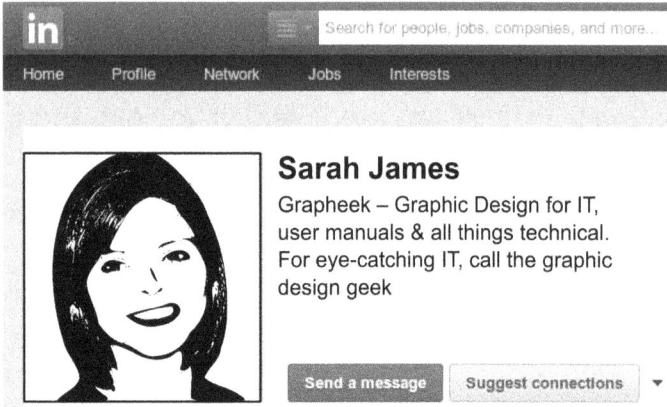

Summary

After performing a search that recognises the keywords you have used, and being impressed by the compelling headline, the prospective client will click on your link. Then, they will be faced with your summary.

The summary is where you run through your experience and achievements. You have 2000 characters to play with, so there's no need to leave out anything that could strengthen your case.

» What to include

Your summary is not about your company, it is about an individual – but always with the business in mind.

Keywords

The same keywords that you came up with for your headline can be incorporated into your summary. This will increase your chances of being found on Google as well as LinkedIn.

Your proposition

To stand out from the crowd you need to provide insight into what you have to offer as an individual.

Evidence

It is easy to write a personal profile using one barren cliché after another, proudly boasting of excellent communication skills and an ability to work under pressure. What really captures the attention of the reader, however, is hard evidence. Emphasise some actual accomplishments, along with relevant names and dates.

Personality

Reveal the character and passion behind the business by providing a bit of background information to explain how and why you came to be doing the work you do.

Call to action

A neat and effective way to end your summary is with a final motivational surge. Entice them with something like: "If you are seeking someone with a passion for {whatever it is you do}, give me a call today."

Contact details

Clients like to have lots of options to make contact, so don't restrict them to communicating via LinkedIn alone. Give them a landline, mobile, email, Skype, postal address, website etc. Then they can use whichever suits them best.

Specialities

This is an efficient way to summarise what you are all about, and reinforce your keywords. Simply list the words that best describe what you have to offer.

» How to write it

Think of your summary like an elevator pitch (as Americans say). It needs to be gripping stuff that won't give readers an opportunity to lose interest and switch off. Here are some tips on how to go about it.

Write in the third person

This is not essential, but the easiest way to blow your own trumpet is to pretend somebody else is blowing it by using 'he' or 'she' instead of 'I'.

Bring it to life

A majority of LinkedIn profiles are utterly soulless and lack emotion. So, don't just provide colourless data, bring it to life and express yourself with real zeal.

Speak like your clients

Keep your language fresh and simple. This means avoiding jargon, unless you are certain that your clients will understand it and expect to see it.

Break it up

A large block of solid text may have some stupendous stuff in it, but it won't get read. Break it up with short paragraphs, subheadings and bullet points, and your key features will stand out and be seen.

Sarah James of Grapheek uses the following summary:

Sarah James

Grapheek – Graphic Design for IT, user manuals & all things technical. For eye-catching IT, call the graphic design geek

[Send a message] [Suggest connections] ▼

You may be brilliant at what you do. You may have developed a wonderful product. But, how are you at communicating it to the rest of us?

Grapheek are experts at presenting technical information in a clear, visual way.

Grapheek make the complex seem simple. They can take a tangle of technical terminology and make it sparkle with clarity. Give them a jumble of instructions and they'll give you a user-friendly user manual.

Formed by Sarah James in 2009, Grapheek is focused on clarifying the often impenetrable world of technology. As Sarah James explains:

"I love all things technical and IT – but tech literature is terrible! Which is why I am on a mission to use my innovative style of graphic design to communicate the wonders of technology in the simplest, clearest way possible – visually (okay, I use some words too)."

In the last year alone Grapheek have helped over 30 clients transform the difficult and dull into the clear and customer-friendly. You can see for yourself at grapheek.com/work

If you want to explain your technology to people that don't speak jargon, contact Grapheek for distinctive graphic design that gets understood. Call 12345 123456

Specialities: Graphic design, IT, technical communications, user manuals, brochures, marketing.

Company page

When a new LinkedIn member submits details for their personal profile, they will be given the opportunity to mention their business. They will then be prompted to create a dedicated company page.

A company page isn't necessary for a sole trader, but for a business wanting to promote a wide range of products and services as well as use LinkedIn for recruitment and other purposes, a company page can be very useful.

To win over visiting prospects, you need to give particular thought to the wording on the company page's banner, description and products and services pages.

Banner

The banner image that appears on a company page provides an opportunity for much more than just a nice picture. It is the perfect place to express skills, demonstrate services and showcase leading product.

You can do this by overlaying the image with text.

For example...

- *Ø* A headline and bullet points
- *Ø* A big bold slogan
- *Ø* Product features
- *Ø* A list of services
- *Ø* User testimonials

...and so on.

The banner image is a chance to highlight your marketing message.

Description

Your description is the first thing people will see when they visit your company page. Whereas your personal profile summary is like a face-to-face chat, your company page description is a tightly focused statement of your company's core proposition.

» State, in brief, what your business is about

Say in clear terms what you do, avoiding extraneous details, such as the company history. You have 1500 characters to play with, but search results typically display only the first 156 characters, so get your key sales proposition into the first 25 words or so.

» Keep it professional

As with the summary, write it in the third person and give your contact details at the end.

» Incorporate your keywords

Most search engines index company pages, so incorporating search terms can lift your page up the Google rankings as well as help you get found within LinkedIn.

Here is Grapheek's company description:

> Grapheek uses graphic design to convey complicated technical information with refreshing simplicity. Perfect for user manuals and all technical and IT communications. Combining expertise in graphic design and a deep understanding of technology, Grapheek helps clients overcome the challenge of technical communications.
>
> For further information, including samples of our work, visit grapheek.com/work or call Sarah James on 12345 123456 for a no-obligation chat.

Showcase pages

This is the sales brochure part of your company page where you can upload text and images to sell your wares. If you already have descriptions written, simply copy them across to LinkedIn. If not, skip along to the Product Descriptions chapter of this book to find out how.

LinkedIn says, "Showcase Pages allow you to extend your Company Page presence by creating a dedicated page for prominent products and services. A Showcase Page should be used for building long-term relationships with members who want to follow specific aspects of your business, and not for short-term marketing campaigns."

To really make the most of LinkedIn's features, you can support your sales message with:

- Individual banner images for your top three products or services, which may incorporate a link to a corresponding web page

- Up to 8 features that appear as bullet points after the description

- Your website address

- A personal contact for further information

- A YouTube video, such as an advertisement or demonstration

- Customised content for different visitors

This last point is pretty amazing, potentially lucrative and woefully underused by the LinkedIn community. A marketing message tailored to suit the specific needs of a particular audience has a much higher chance of making an impact than a one-size-fits-all blurb.

Simply select the 'Create Multiple Variations' option and you can create different versions for different audiences defined by company size, job, industry, seniority or geography.

» Recommendations

When your products or services are recommended by a LinkedIn member, the recommendation is featured on your page, and their network of connections are all notified of the recommendation.

Being recommended, therefore, is a good thing, so you should do all you can to encourage it. So, rather than waiting for satisfied customers to leave recommendations on their own volition, you can get the ball rolling yourself...

- ⊘ Use LinkedIn's Request Recommendations feature to ask customers to leave recommendations (and while you are at it, ask if you can use it elsewhere too, such as on your website)

- ⊘ Invite business associates to leave recommendations

- ⊘ Leave a recommendation for someone else, as etiquette dictates that they will probably reciprocate

❸ GETTING FOLLOWED

As well as making it easier for others to find you, you can take a proactive approach by propelling attractive content outwards to catch the eye of interested members and show them exactly what's so great about your business.

Followers

Followers are people that are so into what you do that they want to receive updates about what you are up to and share it with their own followers. In any other walk of life this would be a bit creepy, but on LinkedIn, it is positively encouraged.

This is because the apparent fan worship of followers has nothing to do with them thinking you are the coolest thing since Justin Beiber. It is simply down to the fact that you may be of use to them. Whether that is by providing insight of some sort or by supplying products and services, it is an opportunity for you to drum up customers, showcase your business, and initiate the occasional piece of viral marketing.

Here are some ways that you can build a following:

- ℗ Request that customers and colleagues from the same business sector follow your page.

- ℗ Add a LinkedIn 'follow' button to your website.

- ℗ Promote your page on other marketing outlets, such as Twitter and emails.

- ℗ Provide content that followers will find relevant, interesting and shareable.

This final method is achieved by sending out a steady supply of Status Updates.

Status Updates

Posting short and interesting status updates on your company page is like placing a tray of freshly baked cookies in the entrance to a shop. Get it right and you will attract people from far and wide. Get it wrong, and you need to rethink your cookie recipe.

Status updates are more likely to be seen than your personal profile, summary, company description and the rest of the pieces you have just been writing because, when you post a status update on your page, it appears on your followers' pages too - putting your message right in front of potential clients.

» What makes a successful Status Update?

Unlike Facebook posts, which build friendly relationships by entertaining people, LinkedIn status updates build business relationships by demonstrating competence in a particular field. To accomplish this, your status updates must be:

Business related

That is, they should address your intended followers' concerns and how you can solve them. For example, they will not be interested that you have taken on a new member of staff, but they will be if your latest recruit has expertise that will be useful to them.

On-brand

Each update should reflect positively on your business, so be careful not to veer off into unprofessional remarks or personal diatribes that have nothing to do with the image you wish to project.

Conversational

There is enough stuff out there on the internet to simply look at or read. What really engages people's interest is something that draws them into an exchange of ideas. Posts that encourage dialogue will gain far more attention than yet another piece of keyword-heavy and value-light writing.

Brief

If you were faced with an update that looked like an essay, would you think: 'Great, I'm gonna sit here for half an hour and read this'? Exactly. If it has to be lengthy, put it elsewhere (such as on your blog) and post an enticing-looking link to it instead.

Regular

If people choose to follow your company page it means they expect a steady flow of updates. If the updates are not forthcoming, they will un-follow you. You can post daily, weekly or monthly, just as long as you post regularly. You should still check daily for any responses to previous posts so that you can answer them without delay.

» What should status updates be about?

Your posts can consist of photos, videos, links or brief pieces of text. Here are some ideas for engaging subject matter:

Your work

A brief update on an interesting project you are working on can demonstrate your competence and remind readers of the type of work you undertake. The subliminal message here is: "This is what I can do for you."

A playground equipment company posted this along with a link to the full story on their website:

> **Perfect Playtime**
> Quite a challenge! How to build a playground for wheelchair users. See how we did it here.
> Like (17) · Comment · Share · 2h ago

Your know-how

Whatever your field of business, share your insights and your expertise and you will attract a grateful and relevant crowd. It doesn't even have to come direct from you. Anything that you encounter that you think could benefit your followers – post it.

A business consultancy posted this along with a link:

> **Better Business**
> This has got to be the best marketing book of the year. Full of fresh insights for the modern world.
> Like (17) · Comment · Share · 2h ago

Your other content

Post a brief and enticing link to introduce and transport the reader to existing content that you have created elsewhere, such as a blog post, case study, video, web page, article, guide or webinar.

An instructor in personal development posts a link to one of his sessions:

> **Personal Power**
> Click here to see video clips of our Sales Communication evening.
> Like (17) · Comment · Share · 2h ago

Industry news

Share any news, related to your industry and you will establish a reputation as an industry expert.

A supplier of office furniture posts this story:

> **Fabulous Furniture**
> I'm back from the Stockholm Office Furniture Fair. Check out these pics of the amazing things I saw.
> Like (17) · Comment · Share · 2h ago

Questions

A good way to build a relationship with your followers is to ask an open question. As well as encouraging debate it could solve a problem that you are experiencing yourself.

A property developer asks:

> **Pride Properties**
> Greenfield or brownfield sites – where would you rather have housing development?
> Like (17) · Comment · Share · 2h ago

Events

Posting an update about a forthcoming event where your business will be exhibiting is a subtle way of saying: "Come and see us face-to-face". It also encourages discussion with fellow attendees.

A retailer of green cleaning products posts:

> **Mean, Clean and Green**
> Exhibiting at the Ideal Home Exhibition for the first time. Any experienced exhibitors got advice?
> Like (17) · Comment · Share · 2h ago

PRESS RELEASES

Grab the headlines and some free publicity into the bargain

If submitting a story to a media outlet so they can write nice things about your business seems almost too easy, why, you may ask, doesn't everybody do it? Well, they do, but most fail.

Getting it right requires mastering different skills and combining them with all the precision of a naked knife juggler unicycling the wrong way round the M25.

Although not as risky (paper cuts aside), a well-crafted press release is an equally effective way to make tomorrow's headlines.

WHAT'S IN THIS CHAPTER?

❶ WHY BOTHER?

Dispatching written announcements to journalists may seem like something from the age of Fleet Street and printing presses – and it is. Press releases have been commonplace since the beginning of the twentieth century.

In our high-tech, ultra-connected digital world, you may think that posting a blog or corresponding via Twitter and Facebook would be a more effective way to get your news out.

While modern methods of communication have their advantages, however, the press release is specifically designed to let us mortals communicate with the big shots in the media and, as a result, the heaps of people who read or watch it.

Why I ❤ press releases

- ❤ When what you have to say in your release matches up with what the editor (it usually is an editor that you deal with) wants to publish, and your target audience matches up with the people that read the editor's publication (it usually is the printed media we are talking about) – then bingo! You've cracked it. You can use a steady flow of press releases to get stories about your products and services in front of the noses of your target market.

- ❤ As they ostensibly come from a third party, your stories carry more credibility than a deliberately placed advertisement or a paid for piece of advertorial.

- ❤ Simply by seeing your business's name in print, potential customers are likely to remember your name and refer you to others.

- ♥ Over time, you can establish yourself as an expert. Be it modern technology, health and fitness or the latest trends in beauty treatments, having your news published marks you out as an authority in your field.

- ♥ A good story that appears in a local newspaper, a trade journal or a niche magazine can get picked up by major media outlets and reworked for a much larger audience. Journalists scour other publications to pick up stories that are relevant to their readership, and so it goes on until you find that your press release has started a news pandemic!

- ♥ Aside from being deployed in the media, a press release can lead a double life as content for a business's website and newsletter. If it is written with SEO (search engine optimisation) in mind – incorporating keywords and website links – and uploaded to an online news hub, a press release will help to drive internet traffic to the website and lift the site higher up the search engine rankings.

- ♥ You can achieve all of this for free – as long as you write them well enough to make an impact. Which is what the rest of this chapter is all about.

Why I ☠ press releases

- ☠ Far too many are bad ones. Ploughing through this endless pile of garbage is a wearisome task to befall any individual. They are lacklustre and display no relevance to the publication or person they have been sent to.

- ☠ Far too many are written by people who don't really get it. A great idea can get filtered down and diluted beyond recognition by someone at a marketing company without the depth of understanding that the actual person behind the story has.

- ☠ They are responsible for the banal, formulaic quotes we see in news stories (*'Reg Smith, Managing Director of Car Parts R Us said: "I am thrilled about our 2-for-1 fan belt offer"'*).

- ☠ 'New media' people are always banging on about the death of the press release. As any editor will tell you from behind a mountain of press releases that have arrived that morning, this is not the case. In fact, new media has breathed new life into press releases, increasing their versatility and power.

The more astute of you may have noticed that these negative aspects of press releases are not problems with the things themselves. They are problems with how they are created and how they are perceived. All of these issues will be dealt with in the pages that follow.

❷ STORY

Without a good meaty news story wrapped up inside it, a press release has all the appeal of a sausage roll without the sausage.

If you don't have a particular story in mind – don't despair! – there are a number of potential headline-grabbers hidden there somewhere. They just need coaxing out.

If you do already have a news story in mind for your press release – hooray! – but read on because you can bet your life that it will benefit from some serious sharpening up so that it grabs the editor's attention like it was written on the side of a tiger.

What editors want

I should warn anyone of a sensitive disposition to brace themselves before reading the next sentence. The fact is, journalists couldn't care less about your business or anyone who works there. It may be the Managing Director's obsession, passion, calling in life – but it is not theirs and, not to put too fine a point on it, they wouldn't give you a glass of water if the entire business were on fire.

The only thing that interests editors and journalists about you is how you can help them.

Give editors what they are looking for
A newsworthy story that their readers will care about.

Instead of newsworthy stories that their readers will care about, editors are hassled all day every day by small businesses giving them stories that are little more than internal memos.

This is because small businesses are utterly wrapped up in the inner workings of their burgeoning enterprise – and they assume everyone else is too. However, like holiday snaps, illnesses and children, other people's are never as interesting as your own.

Unless, that is, they have wider appeal. A holiday snap of you on the beach with Elvis, a narcoleptic bus driver, a child that can predict the winner of the 3:15 at Kempton – now suddenly I'm interested.

The same is true with your business. Editors don't care about your '*2.3% increase in sales over the previous quarter*' but they do when you say that your products are being '*implemented across the NHS to eradicate hospital-acquired infection*'.

So put yourself in the mind of the person that will be reading your news story. What will grab their attention? That is what editors want. Step outside of your business and transform your story into their story.

How to create a news story from absolutely anything (even nothing)

So how can you be sure that yours is the kind of news story that will hit the headlines rather than the bin in the corner of the editor's office?

Here I take three typically lacklustre starting points – promotional hype, a product release and (it doesn't get worse than this) absolutely nothing – and run each through a mechanism that will transform it into a real live bona fide news story.

» Create a news story from… Promotional Hype

Banal marketing clichés, such as Great Low Prices, A Commitment To Quality, Exceptional Customer Service, have been so overused they have ceased to have any impact. Maybe for a fortnight in the late 1950s, we were bowled over by such bravado, but since then, nothing.

Fortunately, a newsworthy story can be fashioned from even the most insipid marketing hype. You just need to extract the interesting stuff that lies behind the promotional fluff. Here's how.

Great low prices!

Why are they so great? Look at the reason why the prices are so low and you will find the kind of story that could attract an editor's eye. Perhaps there is an innovative, cost-cutting method of production. Maybe there are big discounts for special groups (the young, the elderly, the disabled and so on). Or, the business might be run according to the Buddhist principle of doing good rather than maximising profit.

A commitment to quality!

How this will benefit your customer? Be specific. You know what you mean by 'quality' but no one else does unless you spell it out for them. A wine retailer, for example, may insist on only employing staff with a specialist knowledge and years of experience. An IT consultant might offer a free site survey before commencing work and follow it up with a system check-up a month later to ensure everything is operating at optimum efficiency.

Exceptional customer service!

Using a word like 'exceptional' is a big claim, so you need to get across precisely how you go the extra mile for your customers. Do you literally go the extra mile, offering your service to customers no matter how remote they may be (could be a good angle for a mobile shop, pizza delivery or beautician)? Are you a curtain maker that not only measures up and fits the curtains, but brings sample fabrics round to customers' homes to discuss the different options?

Of course, every business is different and has its own particular brand of promotional hype, but you get the idea.

» Create a news story from... A New Product Release

A slightly less-vacuous type of marketing hype is that which surrounds the product release (alternatively, it may be a new service that you are offering).

Imagine that, after months of hard work, a business is finally ready to announce the launch of its exciting new product: the Turbo3000.

To them it is the most momentous event since the invention of the automatic bread slicer. To the rest of us, it isn't so interesting – unless they are a well-known company whose loyal followers have been eagerly awaiting the successor to the Turbo2000 (think of Apple and the release of the latest iPhone).

So what will interest anyone about the launch of the Turbo3000? To uncover the nugget of newsworthiness, you need to imagine yourself being quizzed by an annoyingly inquisitive child:

YOU: "Behold the amazing Turbo3000!"

CHILD: "What's so amazing about it?"

YOU: (rather affronted) "It uses a cantilevered floating counterweight instead of the..."

CHILD: "What does that do?"

YOU: (trying to remain calm) "It makes it significantly lighter and smaller than the old design."

CHILD: "So what?"

YOU: (getting a bit cross) "It can be used in places where previously it could not be used."

CHILD: "Where?"

YOU: (thinking 'shouldn't this child be in school') "Lots of places... wind turbines, aircraft..."

CHILD: "What does it do to them?"

YOU: (getting exasperated) "It makes the rotor operate much more efficiently."

CHILD: "What's so good about that?"

YOU: (about to lose it) Well... a wind turbine would be able to generate more electricity from the same amount of wind."

CHILD: "How much more?"

YOU: (losing it) "10%!!!"

And there we have it. Not a story that interests you – 'The Turbo3000 is here!' – but a story that interests the reader – '10% more electricity from existing turbines'.

» Create a news story from... Absolutely Nothing

If you are starting from scratch, with no obvious news story to publicise, there are still plenty of ways to make the headlines. The solution is found in the ancient Chinese proverb:

TO MAKE THE NEWS, ONE MUST BE THE NEWS

Here's how to be the news:

Be unusual

Rack your brains and think: is there anything out of the ordinary to report about your business? Is the boss a former Olympic medal winner; are there Fancy-Dress Fridays; or is the stationary cupboard haunted?

Be eventful

Organise an event that will draw attention to your services. A café could host a photography exhibition. A graphic design business could organise a 5-aside football tournament between local small businesses. The opportunities are threefold: a press release before the event takes place; networking during the event; and a press release after the event saying what a great success it has been.

Be involved

Look out for any up-coming fairs, festivals or celebrations, and get involved. That way you can muscle in on the event's publicity as well as generate some of your own.

Be first

Being the first at something is always interesting. The first florist in town, the first women-only plumbers, the first person in the area to qualify as a pet hypnotherapist.

Be topical

Keep your eye on the news and you might be able to tie your activities to a ready-made story.

An ongoing news story about the theft of metal due to the high prices it currently fetches provides an opportunity for a company that manufactures a security solution for metal drain covers and the like to get their products mentioned in the press.

Alternatively, you could latch onto something more predictable, like the time of year.

A fitness instructor creates a story about the rush of people wanting to get fit in the build up to summer.

Be trendy

Surveys, website chatrooms and social media provide an ample source of prevailing trends.

A financial advisor notices the growing interest in purchasing buy-to-let properties and decides to share his expert insight using a press release.

Be an expert

Offer authoritative advice on whatever it is people are interested in at the time: '10 Romantic Valentine Gifts', 'Avoid Catching a Cold This Winter', 'Transform Your Garden in a Weekend'... anything that is related to your products or services. Not only does this get you in the news, it marks you out as an expert in your field.

Be generous

Offer free assistance to a local organisation and the local press will want to hear about it.

A chiropodist holds a free *Happy Feet* session for residents at a care home.

An IT Support company conducts a *Get on the 'Net* day at the local library.

Helping the local community gets your business known even before the publicity kicks in. Also, of course, it's just a nice thing to do.

Be heart-warming

If you are making a difference to the life of someone less fortunate than the rest of us – tell us all about it.

A personal trainer improves the life of a cerebral palsy sufferer.

A personal tutor gets a disadvantaged youth into Oxford.

Be different

One way to stand out from the crowd and be newsworthy, is to differentiate your business in such a way that captures the mood of the moment.

A taxi firm in a city that has many other taxi firms gets in the news by being 'the only green taxi firm' - where their cars are especially energy efficient, carbon emissions are offset and cleaning products are environmentally sourced.

After a while, making the news can become a habit, and you won't be able to open a window without calling a reporter and photographer to capture the event.

❸ PRESENTATION

No doubt you are a free-thinking individual with your own ideas and your own way of doing things. A press release, however, is not a place for bohemian free expression.

A press release is constructed according to a precise and inflexible template. Straying from the confines of this time-honoured structure, no matter how agreeable it seems to you, is a way to guarantee failure. So, just this once, keep your rebellious urges in check and play by the rules.

A place for everything

Think of writing a successful press release as like filling in a form. If you were completing a mortgage application form, for example, you wouldn't put an abridged version of your life story in the space allocated for your address, no matter how fascinating your memoirs – because you know that it would not achieve the outcome you desire. The same is true for a press release: fill it in precisely according to what is required in the place it needs to go.

As well as vastly improving your chances of publication, adhering to the familiar format also makes it much easier for you to write. Rather than staring at the emptiness of a blank computer screen for hours on end wondering where to begin, you need only take the standard template and fill in the blanks.

The layout of a typical press release is shown below. We will look at the content of each area later. The positioning of the bits above the headline can differ a little from release to release, and the actual number of 'quote' and 'detail' paragraphs will vary according to what you have to say. Other than that, if it's a press release, this is what it looks like.

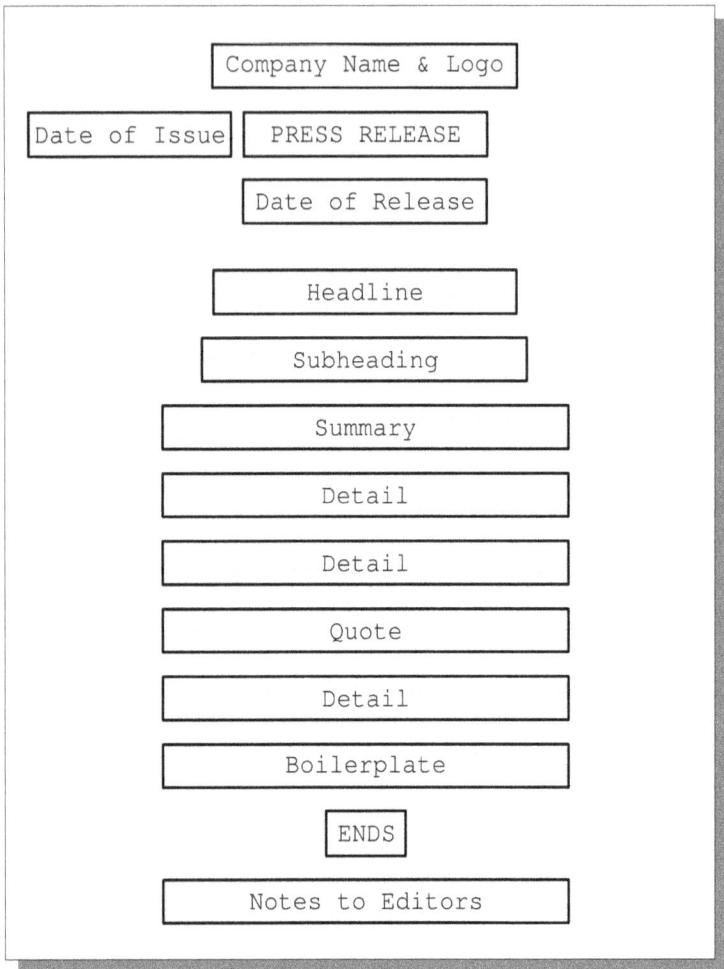

What goes where in a press release

Clarity and simplicity

Free from any clutter and personal indulgences, a press release is clear, consistent and reader-friendly. Its appearance is refreshingly minimal.

You don't need to be a Zen Buddhist to produce a thing of such elegant simplicity, you just need to meditate on the following presentational guidelines:

Font

Keep it simple and clear, such as Times or Arial, and avoid the pseudo mateyness of Comic

Font style

Steer clear of bold, italics and underlining to add emphasis. The editor can decide on that kind of thing. The same goes for bullet points which should only be used if absolutely necessary.

Line spacing

Double space lines if possible to give the editor room to add notes. However, setting line spacing to 1.5 or thereabouts is fine if it allows you to keep the entire release on a single page.

Margins

Set both side margins wide enough to give the editor room to add more notes. 3cm should do it.

Pages

The whole thing should be no more than one page long. If it has to spill onto a second page, put 'continued' at the bottom of the first page.

❹ WORDS

Writing a simple news story using clear facts expressed with straightforward, engaging language is more complex than you might think.

The following tips, techniques and warnings of potential pitfalls will ensure your words are honed and deployed with ninja-like deftness.

What not to write

> *Don't use your press release to sell*
> Press releases are factual, not promotional.

If an editor reading your press release finds it peppered with the sort of empty language described in the following examples, it will be sent binwards before you can say Special Offer!

» A press release is not an advertisement

Most people involved in promoting a business find it hard to ever talk about it dispassionately. This isn't surprising as they are convinced by the worth of their products and services and naturally apply a positive gloss to any words they use when talking about them.

They make unqualified claims, such as something being a 'breakthrough', without there being any supporting evidence. They tell us that it 'will' achieve this or that, as if they had just returned from a trip to the future with their findings. Nouns are preceded by speculative adjectives, such as high quality, new improved or cutting-edge without any justification for why it is high quality, what makes it new improved, and how it is cutting-edge. Editors, however, are made of more cynical stuff and will not be impressed by such unverified hype.

» A press release is not a comedy script

There is a huge temptation to use a press release to share any clever or witty phrases you have dreamt up to describe your business. You must quell that urge, even if it is a beauty like Our hair salon will dye for you. There, look, I couldn't even resist it. Puns and humorous quips are self-indulgent fun that add nothing to your message. So leave them out.

» A press release is not a corporate document

There are few things more irksome than hearing people say things like pushing the envelope, taking it to the next level or mission critical. This management-speak indicates that the speaker is trying to sound more impressive than they actually are. It should, therefore, not be used in a press release.

» A press release is not a technical report

Jargon should only be used when communicating with professionals in the same industry. A press release needs to be understood easily by as many people as possible - so cut out any unnecessary jargon. If the use of some technical terminology is unavoidable, offer a clear, concise explanation of its meaning.

» A press release is not a newsletter

Remember, you are putting yourself in the mind of a journalist, so write using the third person. That means using the name of your business or 'they' instead of words like 'we' or 'I'. Referring to yourself in the third person is a classic sign of narcissism – but you can get away with it in press releases.

Crafting the content

Start at the top of the template shown earlier in this chapter, What goes where in a press release, and work down, pausing at each textual element to fill in the blanks using the techniques described here. Then, watch in thrilled satisfaction as a flawless, irresistible press release materialises before your eyes.

```
             Company name / logo
```

Printing the release onto headed paper gives the editor an instant reference point as well as the assurance of an 'official' dispatch.

```
                PRESS RELEASE
```

It seems obvious but, when it's going to someone who will be surrounded by correspondence of all types, you do not want to set them the task of figuring out what the piece of paper you have sent them is. Put the words 'PRESS RELEASE' centred, bold and in capitals.

```
                Date of issue
```

The date you are sending it out.

```
               Date of release
```

Enter either of the following instructions, in bold and in capitals, to tell the journalist when the story can be released:

FOR IMMEDIATE RELEASE

The story can be used straight away.

EMBARGOED UNTIL xx/xx/xx

The story includes time-sensitive information requiring a deferred publishing date.

Headline

Your headline should be centred, bold and in capitals, or title case if you prefer. Creating it can take as much time as writing the entire remainder of the press release. It's worth it. If the headline doesn't grab them, they won't want to waste any more time on it. A precisely crafted headline crystallises in your mind the specific angle you are taking. Get the headline right and the rest will follow.

With so much at stake, you want to be sure that you get it right. And, using this three-step method for first-rate headlines, you will:

1   What's the story?

    Describe it in one sentence.

2   Cut the waffle.

    Remove every word that is not essential to the story. (You can tell them all the other stuff later. Let's just get them reading it first.)

3   Why is this interesting?

    This is what turns information into an engaging story.

A small business called Street Explorer produces town centre walking guides that incorporate clues to search for as you complete your walk. A guidebook for York has been published and a press release is to be sent out to publicise it.

This is how they arrive at a suitable headline:

1 What's the story?

```
STREET EXPLORER HAVE PUBLISHED A NEW
GUIDEBOOK FOR WALKERS IN YORK
```

2 Cut the waffle

```
NEW GUIDEBOOK FOR WALKERS IN YORK
```

3 Why is this interesting?

The guidebook is interesting because the walkers have to be detectives, hunting for clues. So, by incorporating this into the headline, Street Explorer arrive at:

```
NEW GUIDEBOOK BRINGS DETECTIVES TO YORK
STREETS
```

Compare this final version with that given in the previous two stages. While they would only cause readers' eyes to glaze over, this final headline conjures up an attractive image in the reader's mind that conveys exactly what is newsworthy about the story and compels the reader to read on.

Subheading

Deploying a subheading provides an opportunity to convey supporting information that emphasises and expands on the headline – which frees you to make that headline as sharp, lean and dramatic as is humanly possible.

The subheading should be centred, bold, in sentence case and a point or two larger than the main text if possible. Make every word count by expunging extraneous verbiage (this sentence, for example, should be replaced by 'Keep it simple.')

Street Explorer uses the following subheading:

```
A trail of clues leads walkers
among the city's hidden treasures
```

Summary

The initial paragraph of a press release is not just the first in a sequence of paragraphs, such as you would find in a book or a letter. It is a distinct item in its own right whose function is to furnish the reader with the entire story in a nutshell.

Your first paragraph, therefore, should contain all the pertinent facts and information, so that a reader with absolutely no knowledge of the story can fully grasp what it's all about.

Deciding what to include and what not to include, and assembling it all in the right order, can be tricky... unless you use the interrogation technique.

Imagine that you are sat across the table from a stern looking police constable who wants to know exactly what's gone on or you'll be spending a night in the cells my lad/young lady. If that doesn't work, imagine that you have been dragged in front of a special forces interrogator and he wants answers right now or he'll blow your goddamn head off. That often focuses the mind.

And the questions that require an urgent response are...

What?

Where?

Why?

Who?

How?

When?

As you spill the beans, remember to be concise (your interrogator is not a patient man), crystal clear (or particularly literate) and comprehensive (there is no second chance).

Once you have provided answers to these questions, your interrogator will have sufficient facts to fully understand your news story. You just need to string the answers together in a logical order to form your initial summary paragraph.

Street Explorer begins its release with:

```
A stroll around York city centre has just
become even more enjoyable - with the chance
to follow a trail of clues. It's not a race,
it is purely designed for families, friends,
locals and visitors to uncover fascinating
facts and solve cunning clues as they spend
an entertaining hour or so meandering among
the sights of York. Booklets containing the
clues will be in local shops in time for the
Easter holidays.
```

Details

Here you can expand on the points raised in the summary by adding any supporting details that are relevant to the story.

Typically, you would cover:

- *O* Why (your thing) is better than your competitor's (thing)
- *O* Whom (your thing) is intended for
- *O* Background information about the origins of (your thing)

When you put these details onto the page, remember to...

Pack in all the facts you can muster

Whenever an editor reads a sure-fire fact, a box is ticked inside their head. Facts put the 'news' into news story and consequently, editors love 'em.

Create a new paragraph for each piece of information

A press release isn't a piece of creative writing, it's information. So don't feel the need to use sweeping poetic prose. Just state what is necessary then move on to a new paragraph for the next bit of information, even if it only takes a single, short sentence.

Start with the most important stuff and work down

Press releases do not build to a climax, there is no sting in the tail or dramatic denouement. They start with a bang and get progressively less interesting until they finally fizzle out with some standard blurb which we shall discuss later.

The details of Street Explorer's story look like this:

```
Walkers can begin at any point on the 3km
trail and follow twenty clues that will lead
them back to their starting point.

The pocket-sized booklet, containing clues,
maps and fun facts, will be available from
April 1st at a cost of £2.99 from most local
newsagents.

No prior knowledge is required, just a keen
eye and a sharp mind. And just in case
anyone gets lost, the answers to the clues
can be found at the back of the booklet.

Street Explorer guidebooks are very popular
with larger groups such as birthday get-
togethers, hen parties and corporate days
out, and special group packs containing 10
sets of clues are available exclusively from
www.streetexplorer.co.uk.
```

Quotes

As I have already mentioned, editors love facts. So imagine how excited they get when these facts come straight from the horse's mouth, the Managing Director, for example.

If you do not have a good quote from a suitable person, simply write what it is you want to express and then get their permission to have the quotes attributed to them. Of course, it doesn't have to be the Managing Director, it could be anyone with authority and relevance to the story, such as a technical expert involved in the launch of a new piece of technology.

Rather than just stating the obvious ("This is great") make use of the opportunity to add or underpin a key point ("This is great because..."). And, because you are writing a press release, not a novel, use colons instead of commas to introduce quotes.

A quote from the big cheese at Street Explorer:

```
Street Explorer's Managing Director and
chief clue-setter, Jim Butler, said: "With
over 100 successful guidebooks already
available in towns and cities across the UK,
the enchanting streets of York have provided
us with the most captivating discovery trail
yet!"
```

Boilerplate

When concluding your press release, there is no need to draw things to a close with an 'And finally...', a respectful 'I appreciate you taking the time to read this' or even a simple 'Thank You'. When you have said all you need to say – stop.

Then, drop in a couple of sentences that describe the company. This is often known as a boilerplate (a name given to the durable steel printing plates that were once used over and over again to print repeated blocks of text). This concise description can be reused on all the business's press releases, and probably numerous other places as well.

Large organisations that everyone has heard of do not need to do this as it would not add anything worthwhile to the release. Most other business's, however, do need a boilerplate as who they are is a key element of the story.

The boilerplate for Street Explorer looks like this:

```
Street Explorer was founded in 2010 to give
people the chance to learn more about their
surroundings while enjoying a pleasant urban
stroll. There are currently 105 Street
Explorer guidebooks with more planned for
the future. All products are available from
www.streetexplorer.co.uk
```

ENDS

After the boilerplate comes the 'ENDS' line. Which should be centred and in capitals.

```
- ENDS -
```

This signifies, you guessed it, the end. But not quite.

Notes to editors

Put any practical information, such as contact details, beneath the heading 'Notes to editors', which can be in bold or capitals to help distinguish it from the body copy. Just think of anything that would make life easier for a journalist wishing to pursue your story and provide it here.

I would resist the urge to include extra resources, such as images and video footage. While they can help a journalist to craft their news story, it is best not to send them with the actual release.

The only exception to this is if an image is the story – such as a photograph of Taylor Swift calling by the office to pick up an order in person. In that case, supply photographs that are meaningful and legible.

Otherwise, including resources, either digitally or in hardcopy form, does not help an editor decide whether to run the story or not. It just provides more clutter for them to plough through. Which they won't.

Editors want to be able to scan over a release quickly, and will ask for images, case studies and other supplementary material afterwards if they need them. At this stage, they just want the story. So adding a line to say that images, or whatever, are available on request under the 'Notes to editors' section will be sufficient.

The 'Notes to editors' on Street Explorer's release looks like this:

```
NOTES TO EDITORS

For further information contact: Jim Butler,
Managing Director, Street Explorer.

Tel: 12345 1234567

Email: jbuttler@streetexplorer.com

Available Monday to Friday, 9am to 5pm

Images available on request
```

Here's the complete press release from Street Explorer:

PRESS RELEASE

01/07/2014

FOR IMMEDIATE RELEASE

NEW GUIDEBOOK BRINGS DETECTIVES TO YORK
STREETS

**A trail of clues leads walkers
among the city's hidden treasures**

A stroll around York city centre has just
become even more enjoyable – with the
chance to follow a trail of clues. It's not
a race, it is purely designed for families,
friends, locals and visitors to uncover
fascinating facts and solve cunning clues
as they spend an entertaining hour or so
meandering among the sights of York.
Booklets containing the clues will be in
local shops in time for the Easter
holidays.

Walkers can begin at any point on the 3km
trail and follow twenty clues that will
lead them back to their starting point.

The pocket-sized booklet, containing clues,
maps and fun facts, will be available from
April 1st at a cost of £2.99 from most
local newsagents.

No prior knowledge is required, just a keen
eye and a sharp mind. And just in case
anyone gets lost, the answers to the clues
can be found at the back of the booklet.

Street Explorer guidebooks are very popular with larger groups such as birthday get-togethers, hen parties and corporate days out, and special group packs containing 10 sets of clues are available exclusively from:

www.streetexplorer.co.uk.

Street Explorer's Managing Director and chief clue-setter, Jim Butler, said: "With over 100 successful guidebooks already available in towns and cities across the UK, the enchanting streets of York have provided us with the most captivating discovery trail yet!"

Street Explorer was founded in 2010 to give people the chance to learn more about their surroundings while enjoying a pleasant urban stroll. There are currently 105 Street Explorer guidebooks with more planned for the future. All products are available from streetexplorer.co.uk.

- ENDS -

NOTE TO EDITORS

For further information contact: Jim Butler, Managing Director of Street Explorer.

Tel: 12345 1234567

Email: jbuttler@streetexplorer.com

Available Monday to Friday, 9am to 5pm

Images available on request

❺ DISPATCH

Like a mega-rocket on Guy Fawkes Night, a press release must be launched with careful timing on a precise bearing to achieve optimum impact on the intended audience.

Get it slightly wrong and your audience will be left unmoved as the spectacle takes place out of sight. Get it very wrong and your garden shed goes up in flames, metaphorically speaking.

So stand well back, keep your pets indoors, and read on to discover how to make your press release go with a bang.

Target your publication

There has never been as many potential recipients for your news, so why not make the most of your press release and spread your news around?

Newspapers (local and national, daily and weekly), magazines, trade journals, online outlets, broadcasters (radio and television, local and national)... Within each sector lie countless individual publications and outlets; and within each of these you will typically find a number of specialist sections, features and inserts, each produced with a tightly defined demographic in mind. Where this demographic tallies with your intended audience is where you need to send your press release.

A business manufacturing parts for vintage radios sends press releases to The Vintage Wireless Society Bulletin. Though this has a tiny readership compared to, say, The Sun newspaper, it will reap a greater reward as its readership will be interested in what they have to say.

For the same reason, a business manufacturing sexy bras gets a better response from sending their press releases to The Sun rather than The Vintage Wireless Society Bulletin.

Think creatively when considering who your target market actually is...

A mobile massage service sends press releases to the Lifestyle section of a local newspaper. They also promote the same service with a press release sent to the Business section suggesting a story about how "massage in the workplace relieves stress and increases productivity".

If you are sending your release to more than one media outlet, write individually tailored submissions that are tightly focused on each one's particular area of interest.

Target your editor

So you know the organisation(s) that you intend to send your release to, but what about the actual person on whose desk you want it to land?

Address it to *Interior Design Monthly* and your masterpiece will most likely be 'dealt with' by the receptionist. Send it to *The Editor* and you run the risk of it being overlooked due to the sheer number of editors of one form or other that populate these workplaces.

You need to address your press release directly to the individual who is responsible for preparing the publication or specific section that you want to target, and do so using their proper title and spelling their name correctly.

To do this you can either:

- *O* Look for an editorial staff listing in the publication.
- *O* Look for one on their website.
- *O* Get hold of their directory or yearbook, possibly from your local library. Larger media organisations often publish these (and what you may think of as a small outfit could be part of a larger organisation).
- *O* Give them a ring. When the receptionist answers, say you want to send a press release in for whatever section and you would like the name of the appropriate editor.

Then it is just a matter of determining their preferred method for receiving the release.

How to send it

Most media outlets' websites contain clear instructions on how to submit a press release. If not, often there will be a phone number for each department. Simply ring the relevant number and ask how they prefer to receive their releases.

By post

Many organisations prefer to receive press releases the traditional way: through the postal system. In this case, simply print off your release, pop it in a stamped addressed envelope, say a prayer, then send it off.

Online

Most local newspapers have an online form for you to simply copy and paste your release into.

By email

If the recipient is happy to receive releases via email, there are a number of pros and cons to consider:

- ✓ It costs you nothing.

- ✓ It is faster than snail mail.

- ✓ It is easy for a journalist to copy and paste your text straight into their document, edit it, then run it.

- ✗ It may well be considered spam and automatically directed into a junk folder (I know it shouldn't, but it probably will).

- ✗ An editor's inbox can get flooded by hundreds of messages, not just press releases, and it is very easy for them to put their finger on the delete key and leave it there until the problem has disappeared.

The best way to overcome these possible hitches is to ring first and say that you are concerned about being considered spam. Hopefully they will be able to put your mind at rest. Also, a call like this can also be a good way to get your release noticed.

When creating the email to transmit your masterpiece, follow these guidelines:

- ℗ Paste your text into the body of the e-mail rather than include a link or attachment. No one opens an attachment these days unless they can be absolutely, positively, without-a-shadow-of-a-doubt certain it does not contain a virus.

- ℗ Use plain text. HTML and other sophisticated extras will add odd characters and unexpected formatting to your release.

- ℗ Start the subject line with 'RELEASE:', then follow with something short and interesting. If your existing headline is too long, use it as the starting point and boil it down to the essence of the story.

O Address one email to one editor. If you are emailing more than one, do them individually so they all feel special.

Street Explorer email their press release using the subject line:

```
RELEASE: Detectives Hit York Streets
```

When to send it

As with comedy and boiled eggs, timing plays a crucial part in the success or otherwise of a press release.

O If it is topical, a swiftly written and dispatched release is essential.

O Avoid sending your press releases out during the three weeks surrounding Christmas and New Year, unless you have relevant festive news to announce.

O Don't dispatch your release just before the contact person named under 'Notes for editors' disappears on holiday. The spokesperson, must be available to speak to a journalist in case they want to follow up the story.

O The best day of the week to send out a press release? Most observers say that it doesn't matter. Even so, I prefer to send them off on a Monday or Tuesday as it avoids the Bermuda Triangle effect where all physical evidence and mental recollection of a press release vanishes over the weekend.

What to do after you have sent it

Once you have released your release, don't follow it up the next day with a phone call to see if they have received it.

This would achieve nothing, except aggravate the already harassed journalist, which is a sure-fire way to sabotage your efforts. However, if you have heard nothing after a couple of days or so, you could give them a ring. If nothing else, this might provide you with some insight into what went wrong (maybe you mistyped the address, maybe they covered a similar story last issue, maybe the editor used your press release to rest his coffee mug on...).

The spokesperson should be prepared to chat to a journalist about your story if they get in touch. It's also a good idea to have a 'press kit' prepared in advance that includes any additional relevant material, such as photographs, that they may require.

When sending any information like this, write the words 'Requested Information' on the subject line (if an email) or next to the address (if posted).

PRODUCT
DESCRIPTIONS

Convey desirability in catalogues,
brochures, e-commerce...

Whether they are to appear in catalogues, brochures, websites, flyers, advertisements or labels attached to the products themselves, product descriptions do much more than simply describe.

They give the product a voice.

They bring it to life.

They reach out to the customer, grab them by the lapels and give them a big kiss on the lips.

WHAT'S IN THIS CHAPTER?

❶ MARKETING MATCHMAKING

You have the right product and the right consumer, but unless there is the right chemistry between the two, they will pass each other by like ships in the night.

Creating the bond that brings them together is like arranging a blind date: you must be well acquainted with both parties before you can create a successful encounter.

The product

"I'm different from all the rest"

Figuring out what your product's got that others do not have is the starting point of an appealing and persuasive product description. Marketing people call it the product's USP, its unique selling proposition. This is what makes it special, what differentiates it from similar products, what makes it a viable offer.

For this reason, don't be tempted to do a blanket reproduction of the product description supplied by the manufacturer. Everyone will do that. You need to make yours stand out from the crowd, especially on the web where you are rubbing shoulders with your competitors.

The customer

"I'm looking for love at first sight"

While one product description may leap out at a reader, causing them to punch the air and exclaim, "Yes! This is the one for me," a different description of the same product may leave them unmoved. This is because, like beauty, the USP is in the eye of the beholder.

The more you understand your target market, the more you can address their specific desires. That is, you need to know what tickles the fancy of your prospective consumer before you can write a product description or consider how it is presented and where it will appear.

The perfect couple

"A match made in marketing heaven"

Using your understanding of the product and the customer, you can create a description that brings the two into perfect alignment.

Without this mutual understanding, you may as well write the description in Swahili. You can even use a range of different descriptions for the same product to tap into a range of different markets.

Gourmet-to-Go are an online business supplying the kind of foodstuff unavailable in typical supermarkets. They want a product description for their pack of Artisan Cheeses, but first they need to consider what the pack has to offer each discerning market:

• Cheese connoisseurs seek distinctive flavours from around the world.

• Healthy eaters want to know whether it is organic, what its fat content is, whether it is free from artificial colours, flavours and additives.

• Those with special dietary requirements need to know about specific ingredients, whether it is Kosher, Halal etc.

• Gift buyers are attracted by its presentation and packaging.

...and so on.

As a result of these well-defined relationships between different markets and different attributes, the description used in an advertisement placed in Cheese Enthusiast magazine, for example, would take a very different tack to one placed in a Christmas Gifts catalogue.

❷ CONTENT

What you have to say about a product can be divided into two categories: features and benefits. The two are as incontrovertibly linked as an electric drill (feature) and the hole it makes (benefit).

Features

When you ask a manufacturer to describe a product, they will most likely begin by telling you about its physical attributes: from the revolving flange mechanism at the top to the self-locking castors at the bottom. They will then go on to provide detailed dimensions, precise colour references and a step-by-step account of the manufacturing process that brought the product into being. These are the features.

> *Features are all about the product*
> Assume your reader knows nothing about the product. Tell them every detail.

Books-for-Cooks produce limited edition cookery books for small, local markets. Their latest publication, The Kent Coast Cookbook, includes recipes involving local seafood. The book's features are:

• Local seafood recipes

• When and where to buy seasonal ingredients

• Spiral-binding

• Laminated pages

• Step-by-step instructions

Benefits

When you ask the user of the product to describe it, they will tell you what it does for them: how it has made things better, faster, slower, easier, cheaper, more enjoyable, more comfortable, less stressful… all the ways it has improved their life. The mere sight or touch of it may brighten their day. Its quality and reliability may give them peace of mind. These are the benefits.

> *Benefits are all about the customer*
> Assume your reader has never used the product. Let them know all the things that are good about using it.

As the whole point of writing the description is to sell the product to customers, it is the benefits that have most influence. But how can you wax lyrical about benefits when all you know are features? Fortunately, features lead to benefits like wardrobes lead to Narnia.

The Kent Coast Cookbook's previously mentioned features lead to the following benefits. Books-for-Cooks will emphasise these benefits when promoting the book:

- Local seafood recipes allow readers to eat healthily and support local businesses
- Knowing when and where to buy seasonal ingredients makes it easy to get what you need and pre-empts disappointment arising from seafood that is out of season
- Spiral-bound pages remain open at the right page
- Laminated pages wipe clean
- Step-by-step instructions are fool-proof, ensuring you get the recipe right first time

More benefits

Unearthing a whole load of tempting benefits for your product can sometimes feel like digging for pirate treasure without a map – and not knowing what that treasure would look like even if you did find it.

By using the following method, however, you can equip yourself with more than enough benefits to beguile the most hard-to-please reader.

What's the point of {insert your product here}?

Take each individual feature, as well as the product as a whole, sit it down and ask it to justify its existence. Don't be afraid to go overboard with your answers, you can always rein things in later.

- What problem does it solve?
- What outcome does it make possible?
- Can it do more of what it does, or do it faster, better…?
- How does it do what it does better than the alternatives?
- Who could benefit from it?
- What occasions would it be used?
- Whereabouts could it be used?
- How will its feel/smell/sound/touch/taste impact on the user?
- How will using it make the user feel?
- What can it be used with?
- How is it made in a way that the user will appreciate?
- Why is it such good value for money?

Once you have supplied answers to these questions, assemble the ones that will most strike a chord with your target reader into a logical flow – and there you have the makings of a benefit-led product description.

The Kent Coast Cookbook's product description conveys to the reader that it is much more than just a book of recipes.

The Kent Coast Cookbook

Discover local culinary delights with this unique and practical guide to regional seafood dishes

The Kent Coast Cookbook is the perfect way to savour the delights of fresh, local seafood. Packed with regional recipes that are good for you and good for the local fishing community, it also gives you a handy What, When, Where buying guide to seasonal ingredients – so you'll never miss the boat!

Splatter-proof pages

Robust spiral-bound pages sit open at the page you are using, so you won't lose your place mid-recipe. And you don't need to worry about splashes or tears as all pages have a strong, wipe-clean laminated finish. Enjoy these recipes again and again – and the book stays like new.

Easy-to-follow instructions

Whether you're a complete beginner or a skilled cook, you'll be inspired by the extensive range of mouth-watering recipes. With fool-proof instructions and helpful illustrations, The Kent Coast Cookbook is the ideal companion whether you're cooking for yourself, your family or hosting a banquet.

---

❸ OOMPH

Once you have devised the appropriate wording to describe your product's features and benefits, ask yourself: Does it wow? Does it woo? Does it sing in the customer's ear like a nightingale? Does it sparkle like a thousand diamonds in the sun? Does it have oomph?

Thought not. Read on.

Perk up features

There can be so much more to features than a list of bullet points, especially when a picture is involved, which it almost always is. Illustrate your product with an image that is large, clear and (this is a great one if you can do it) shows the product in use. This gives you the opportunity to present your features in ways that stimulate interest and increase impact. The most common methods are call-outs, icons, captions and panels.

» Call-outs

Short pieces of text outside of a picture with a line or arrow linking it to the relevant section of the image.

» Icons

Symbols placed on the product's image with an accompanying key explaining each symbol's meaning can reduce and simplify otherwise long-winded descriptions. Another option is numbered bullets that correspond to numbers on the picture.

» Captions

A caption beneath an image used to demonstrate a feature will put the picture in context and convey the pertinent information ahead of any mention of it in the main description.

» Panels

Supplementary elements of a description, such as definitions, additional information or alternative options, can be pulled out from the main text and presented in a separate panel. This leaves the remaining text undiluted by extraneous information. As long as you keep their numbers under control, presenting features in panels makes it easier for the reader to understand and more likely that they will read them in the first place.

Here are all four methods shown in action – though if you combine them all like this you are likely to confuse the reader and probably yourself. Best to choose a system that suits your product and stick with it.

Panels allow you to provide a detailed exposition of secondary information without it interfering with the primary message

Callouts enable you to point to the thing that you are talking about

★ Icons are great when a feature occurs in multiple locations

A caption helps to explain the image

Bring benefits to life

As somebody once said (probably a sausage salesman), "Sell the sizzle, not the sausage." By which they were suggesting that the key feature of a sausage is a cylinder of indeterminate pig meat – but the benefit to the buyer is a tasty breakfast sizzling in the pan, the aroma wafting across the kitchen, the… etc. etc.

So, how do you say it with sizzle?

» Put the reader in the picture

Don't try to bowl the reader over with overconfident sales talk or in-house jargon. Write as if you are speaking to them personally. Build a rapport with your reader by imagining yourself in their position, showing empathy and using 'you' (rather than 'the customer', for example) when describing benefits.

IMPERSONAL:

"DataDay backup has remote access."

PERSONAL:

"You can access your DataDay backup wherever you are in the world."

» Tap into their aspirations

Tell the reader how your product will give them what they desire. By writing for the readers' personality and the goals they aspire to, your words will stimulate the reader into imagining themselves with your product.

A pottery business that creates imprints of babies' and toddlers' hands knows exactly what their target market – mums – want:

Those tiny hands grow too soon and memories begin to fade. Capture this fleeting moment in your child's life in clay and you will have a memory to treasure for the rest of your life.

» Be specific

When saying what your product does, be precise. Remember, you are addressing individuals, not a group, so don't talk in generalisations.

GENERIC:

"Perfect for containing all kinds of things around the home."

SPECIFIC:

"Perfect for tidying toys, packing papers, storing shoes etc."

» Tackle possible resistance head-on

If the reader has a doubt about the product, no amount of upbeat swagger is going to remove it from their mind. The only way do deal with doubt is to raise any possible reservations yourself and deal with them directly.

An architect knows that his clients may be concerned that he will be flitting between different jobs, unable to immerse himself in their project, so he puts their mind at rest:

I take care not to spread myself too thinly, so you can be sure of a first class, professional job with no delays or distractions.

» Use evocative adjectives

Don't use the same, generic adjectives all the time, especially if you are writing descriptions for a number of products, because they soon become ineffective. A compelling word that conveys precisely how a product will improve a reader's life will resonate with them in a way that a weak, imprecise one will not. If you are struggling, use the thesaurus on your PC.

INSIPID:

"Make great presentations"

INSPIRING:

"Make captivating presentations"

» Give it zip

Your writing must be easy for the reader to understand and respond to positively. Grab their attention from the first word, break up lengthy descriptions with subheadings that highlight key benefits and use sentences that are crisp and compact. Make every word count and keep the overall tone active, not passive.

PASSIVE:

"The use of bicycles amongst the general population is rising year on year."

ACTIVE:

"More people ride bicycles."

» Make your headline count

More people read the headline than read the description, so it is worth spending time to get it right. A simple product name will not cut the mustard. Your headline is an opportunity to grab the readers' attention, put the main user-benefit up there in big letters and inspire them to read on. You may find it easier to compile your description then come back to the headline afterwards, when you have a clearer idea of what your key message actually is.

UNINTERESTING:

"Garden Gate"

INTRIGUING:

"Secure your garden... Beautifully"

» Use tech specs

With technical products, knowledgeable users may be looking for specific features to compare to similar products. Terms like 100GB, Teflon Coated or G3-S Custom Shocks, need little explanation to those in the know. The mention of the feature is enough to trigger the benefit in the mind of the tech-savvy customer. In this situation, features should be given prominence, though the benefits can still be spelled out more clearly for the not so clued-up customers.

» Consider online searches

When a product description is to appear on a website, the spectre of SEO (search engine optimisation) raises its interfering head. Relevant search terms must be used in the description and in the title, ideally. However, as is described in more detail in the Website chapter, text that is relevant and readable will be ranked higher than meaningless text crammed with keywords. If your description is to appear on a page designed around a specific search term, relevant keywords should occur naturally as you write.

» Clarify buying information

Specific price details and instructions on how to make a purchase are not part of the product description itself. They should, however, accompany the description and leave the reader in no doubt about what they need to do to get their hands on the item you have described so irresistibly.

Fine-tune presentation

The step from feature to benefit is not a single discrete jump, it is a gradual progression. This allows you to present your description in a spectrum of possible styles – from full-on features to out-and-out benefit bonanza – as illustrated by the Features-Benefit-O-Meter.

» The Features-Benefit-O-Meter

The following example shows how the same product can be described in different ways by slowly turning the dial on the Features-Benefit-O-Meter from one end of the scale to the other.

An IT retailer wants to promote the So-Ho Printer, designed with the self-employed in mind, with special features that enable large-scale printing jobs to be carried out in the small office and home office (hence: So-Ho).

(For simplicity, basic features are shown as bullet points – this does not have to be the case. Also, the full list of technical specifications that would normally follow each description has been omitted.)

100% FEATURES / 0% BENEFITS

So-Ho Printer

- Paper shelf
- Printout guide
- Receiving tray

75% FEATURES / 25% BENEFITS

So-Ho Printer

- Slideable paper shelf
- Wire printout guide
- Printout receiving tray

50% FEATURES / 50% BENEFITS

So-Ho Printer

- Paper shelf slides forward for easy paper loading
- Wire guide routes printouts to the front for collection
- Receiving tray ensures printouts are neatly stacked

25% FEATURES / 75% BENEFITS

So-Ho Printer

The So-Ho Printer incorporates a handy shelf that glides forward to allow large stacks of paper to be loaded with ease. Printouts slip smoothly along a wire guide to the front ready for collection. And, thanks to a 150-sheet receiving tray, your printouts can be stacked without jams, overflows or creasing.

0% FEATURES / 100% BENEFITS

Home-Office Printing That Means Business

Tired of loading paper, unravelling paper jams, picking printouts off the floor and hearing that annoying beep that means there's yet another printer error to deal with? Well, now you can forget about jams, overflows and fault-finding and enjoy the effortless efficiency of a first-class business printer in your small or home-office.

Hard-working and effortless to use

Loading the So-Ho Printer is a breeze. A shelf glides out to accept a stack of paper, then retracts to install it automatically. High quality printouts slip smoothly along a wire guide to the front, where they enter a receiving tray that stacks the crisp, clean pages ready for you to collect. And, with a 150-page capacity, you can leave the So-Ho to get on with printing while you get on with what you do best.

Compact and cost-effective

If you're thinking that a machine like this must be big and expensive, think again. The So-Ho Printer is designed for the smaller office – and it has a size and price tag to match.

Of course, even in this last '100% benefits' example, features are not absent. They act as the hook on which to hang the all-important benefits.

SALES LETTERS

**Craft correspondence that
compels readers to react**

An exquisitely crafted, one-page sales letter is a thing to behold.

The simplicity of its construction, the precision of its composition and the efficiency of its narrative as it elegantly unravels over the course of a single page combine in a tour de force that is part modernist masterpiece and part customer catnip.

What's in this Chapter?

❶ BETTER LETTERS

There are two types of sales letter: appealing ones, that make a genuine personal connection with the reader; and appalling ones, that make an unprovoked assault on the reader.

Here are the ground rules for ensuring your letter is as appealing to your readers as honey is to Winnie the Pooh.

Solve a problem

Why are you writing this letter? If you reply with something like, 'To get more customers,' or, 'To publicise my products,' you need to consider the two essential rules of sales letter subject matter.

> *The two essential rules of sales letter subject matter*
> Rule 1: Keep it reader-centric. Define your objective around the needs of the customer, not what you want to say.
> Rule 2: Keep it specific. Express your objective in a few, simple words, not a vague, catch-all aspiration.

When the purpose of your letter sticks to these two rules, you will be writing something the reader actually wants to read about. If your letter does not have a specific objective relating to the reader's personal experience, it will be of as much relevance and interest to them as your gas bill.

This is summed up in the following piece of time-honoured marketing wisdom:

> ## 'Tell me about my lawn, not your grass seed'

Taking this literally, what would you rather read about in a letter selling grass seed:

What matters to the manufacturer…

"Our grass seed was devised in our £2million laboratory in Milton Keynes where it was genetically engineered by our scientists for cultivation with a 60% lower water requirement and to resist the spread of weeds under a variety of conditions."

…or what matters to you?

"How would your family spend summer on a lush green lawn? Playing games, enjoying barbecues with friends, relaxing in the sun with a cool drink? Whatever you choose to do, less watering and weeding gives you more time to make the most of those precious summer days."

Don't sound weird

Remember that you are writing a letter, not an advertisement. It's almost the same as speaking with someone in person. So, unless you are in the habit of walking up to prospective clients and saying:

"BUY NOW!"

or,

"YOU'D BE MAD TO MISS THIS KRAAAAZY OFFER!"

don't write your letters like that.

Instead, picture yourself having a level-headed conversation with the reader – and when I say 'the reader' I mean a single individual, don't talk as if you were addressing a group. Adapt your style of language to match theirs, just as you would in normal conversation.

To make sure your letter sounds like one written by a human being (rather than some hyped-up marketing machine), read it aloud to someone stood right in front of you. If it sounds a bit weird, it is.

Follow the format

There is a natural, logical sequence to writing a sales letter. Whatever your proposition, stick to this format and it will unfold before your readers' eyes with such effortless elegance they will almost hear a 'Ta-daa!' when they reach the bottom of the page.

Despite what you would imagine from reading the ads for some tuition books and websites on the subject, there is no trickery or covert hypnotic techniques involved. And there is nothing mystical about the format (though I did discover it written in code on the back of a Leonardo Da Vinci canvas). It is simply a way to express yourself with absolute clarity.

This winning format is shown in the following diagram, 'What goes where in a sales letter'. Don't worry about the wording in each box at the moment, we'll come to that next.

```
┌─────────────────────────────────────────┐
│                        ┌──────────────┐  │
│                        │    Your      │  │
│      ┌──────────────┐  │   Address    │  │
│      │    Their     │  └──────────────┘  │
│      │   Address    │  ┌──────────────┐  │
│      └──────────────┘  │    Date      │  │
│    ┌───────────────────────────────┐     │
│    │          Headline             │     │
│    └───────────────────────────────┘     │
│      ┌─────────────────────────────┐     │
│      │      Headline Group         │     │
│      └─────────────────────────────┘     │
│   ┌──────────────┐                       │
│   │   Greeting   │                       │
│   └──────────────┘                       │
│    ┌───────────────────────────────┐     │
│    │          Problem              │     │
│    └───────────────────────────────┘     │
│    ┌───────────────────────────────┐     │
│    │          Solution             │     │
│    └───────────────────────────────┘     │
│    ┌───────────────────────────────┐     │
│    │          Benefits             │     │
│    └───────────────────────────────┘     │
│    ┌───────────────────────────────┐     │
│    │         Motivation            │     │
│    └───────────────────────────────┘     │
│    ┌───────────────────────────────┐     │
│    │        Reassurance            │     │
│    └───────────────────────────────┘     │
│    ┌───────────────────────────────┐     │
│    │        What To Do             │     │
│    └───────────────────────────────┘     │
│    ┌───────────────────────────────┐     │
│    │          Summary              │     │
│    └───────────────────────────────┘     │
│   ┌──────────────┐                       │
│   │   Sign Off   │                       │
│   └──────────────┘                       │
│    ┌───────────────────────────────┐     │
│    │         Postscript            │     │
│    └───────────────────────────────┘     │
└─────────────────────────────────────────┘
```

What goes where in a sales letter

❷ WORDS

Writing a sales letter is not like writing to your Auntie (unless you are trying to sell stuff to your Auntie, in which case, shame on you). It is like working your way down a checklist, creating blocks of text as you go.

You can edit and combine them afterwards, but for now, just give each block of text everything you've got.

Letter content

`Headline`

The reader will read the headline before anything else. The headline grabs attention, sets the scene and gives the reader a very good reason why they need to stop what they are doing right now and read your letter. The headline is the most important part of the letter, so it's worth spending plenty of time on it.

You want a headline that...

Can't be missed

Rather than being 'read', the best headlines are 'assimilated', instantly absorbed by the viewer whether they want to or not. Like a road sign or a poster for a film, they have an intense simplicity that you just can't help but take in. Anything half-hearted won't cut the mustard. You need a headline that hits the reader like a frying pan on the head (but in a nice way).

Can't be ignored

Once glimpsed, the headline should compel the reader to read on. The unequivocal benefits of doing so must be made blatantly clear. (Beware going overboard, however. If you entice the reader by promising the Earth, only to deliver the Isle of Wight, they will feel let down.)

Your headline should be located about one quarter of the page down from the top (giving you room for addresses etc.). It doesn't matter if it is in upper, sentence or title case, but it should typically be centred and bigger and/or bolder than the rest of the text.

» How to create the perfect sales letter headline

The following laboratory-tested method will result in a headline that couldn't create more interest if it had a lit fuse coming from it.

1   Put yourself in the mind of the reader

Unlike many forms of marketing, the sales letter is targeted at a specific individual. You know who they are. You know all about them. So do a bit of method acting and 'become' the reader for a while, and look at the world from their perspective.

2   Find the benefit

While you are in your reader's mind, you will notice that they care less about the features and specifications of what you are offering and more about what it can do for them. You need to pin down how your product or service will benefit the person receiving the letter. And you do that by completing this magic phrase:

"With {this product or service}, you will be able to…"

Whatever you say to complete this sentence is the benefit. And this is what your headline is all about.

A letter promoting the services of Action IT, a technical support company, to local businesses requires a headline. So the letter writer says the magic phrase.

'With our IT services, you will be able to...'

and they complete the sentence with:

'...get on with your work without worrying about costly IT problems.'

3 Turn the benefit into a headline

The benefit may come out as a fully formed headline, but chances are it will need a bit of refining. Here are some ways you can phrase the headline to give maximum emphasis to the benefit. Adapt your benefit into each of the following styles of headline to see which works best.

Promise something:	How to...
	Unlock the secret of...
	Free...
Tantalise the reader:	Imagine...
	You could be...
	What if...
Offer a challenge:	Experience...
	Discover...
	Learn...
Ask a question:	Tired of...?
	Are you spending more on...?
	Do you still...?
Impress with facts:	Special report...
	8 out of 10 businesses...
	75% of PCs are...
Assert possibilities:	For £10 you can...
	In one week you could...
	You can become...

Action IT turn their benefit ("With our IT services you will be able to get on with your work without worrying about costly IT problems.") into a headline by asking the reader:

Could your business survive an IT failure?

4 Beware gimmickry

Humour can be used in the headline – but only if it actively engages the reader, rather than just used for the sake of it. The same is true of puns. Unless, it is relevant – such as the plumbing business which uses the following headline to announce its rapid leak-repair service...

Drip, Drip, Hooray!

...wordplay will just get in the way of the pure, unadulterated message you wish to convey. Similarly, fancy fonts, wavy text, clip art, multi-colours – they all distract from what your headline is saying. So steer clear and let the words speak for themselves.

5 If it can't all be said in the headline

In most cases, shorter headlines are best, ideally between 5 and 12 words. Reading a headline this length requires no effort whatsoever on the part of the reader. However, if it can't be said in a just a few words you could try a 'headline group' (not to be confused with U2 at Glastonbury).

Headline group

A headline group is a headline plus a bit more beneath, usually in a smaller font size. The extra bit can be used to refer to anything that will add further impetus to the headline, such as an offer of some kind.

The headline group may be involve another sentence or it may be a short bulleted list. It doesn't matter as long as it is as tightly focused on the customer-benefit as the main headline.

Action IT bolster their headline with a hint at the solution on offer:

Could your business survive an IT failure?

Just because you don't have an IT department
doesn't mean you can't have complete IT support

A well-targeted business owner reading this headline would not be able to avoid reflecting on the catastrophic costs and mayhem resulting from a broken IT system – and would feel compelled to read on to discover the solution.

Compare this level of engagement to the indifference generated by the kind of headline that is not based on the needs of the customer:

We are technical support specialists

Exactly. Who cares?

Greeting

Like any conversation, the first words you convey in your letter will set the tone for the rest of the exchange. Whether your letter is to be read by someone that you are on first name terms with, or someone that you wouldn't know if they were sat on your lap, it should always begin with a greeting that is friendly and polite.

Use their name

'Dear Mrs. Robinson' will make more of an impact than 'Dear Sir/Madam' or 'Dear Managing Director'. So if you have or can get hold of their actual name, use it.

Be sincere

As comic legend Bob Monkhouse said: "The secret of success is sincerity. Once you can fake that, you've got it made." Sincerity in your letter is absolutely essential to its success. Don't guess at a spelling or gender if you don't know it. Find out. That's what the internet is for.

If all else fails

When you simply absolutely can't find the correct name or form of address there are other options that enable you to begin your letter.

Option A... Forgo the greeting altogether. Rather than risk getting it wrong, just dive in there, straight into the body of the letter, without any greeting. If your headline and opening sentence are effective enough, the reader will be too caught up in the flow to notice.

Option B... Write something personal instead. Something short and friendly. As if you know the reader but have no need to actually use their name:

> I hope you don't mind me getting in touch, but I think you might be interested in what I have to offer...

Or, if appropriate, a short attention-grabber that tells the reader that this is something specially for them:

> Attention all busy mothers!

Or, better still, something more personal:

> As someone working in haulage, I thought you'd like this

Option c... Do what everybody else does.

These openers are neither friendly or polite, and they certainly aren't personal – but loads of businesses use them.

> Dear Customer...

> Dear Subscriber...

> Dear Sports Lover...

I don't like this kind of 'welcome'. If you want your letter to be better than the dross that most businesses send out, ignore this point and choose either (a) or (b) instead. Better still, tear (c) out and bin it (after first reading the other side of the page and committing it to memory).

Having said that, it is occasionally possible to use a humorous non-personal greeting to show that you understand the readers' pain.

A web hosting company writes to businesses, beginning their letter with:

Dear Overcharged Website Owner,

Action IT use a combination of a purchased mailing list and a little research into local businesses using the internet to obtain the name of the person that is able to make a decision about IT maintenance, usually the Managing Director.

Dear Mrs. Barker,

Problem

After the 'Dear Whoever', what is the most natural thing to write? Probably something along the lines of: "I am writing to you about...".

Well, firstly, I already know you are writing, I'm reading the damn thing. And secondly, why should I care what you are doing? I don't even know who you are. So, best not to open with that.

Instead say something about the reader. More specifically, raise something that concerns them: a worry of theirs, a nuisance, a fear, that you alluded to in the headline. Try to bring it alive in their minds and show that you really understand how they feel.

A property investment company knows that their key prospects' are people looking to escape from the 9-5 rat race:

Are you tired of the daily grind? Working all hours for little reward while your life passes you by?

Action IT have raised the fear of an IT failure in their headline. Then, rather than a straightforward statement like:

What would you do if your computers crashed?

they emphasise what the problem actually is – delays and loss of income while the system is repaired:

Nothing wastes time and money in business like computer downtime, especially when there's no IT department to come to the rescue.

A brief reference to their fears will focus readers' minds. You can then move onto how you can help them.

Solution

You've set up the problem, now you can introduce the solution. At this stage, you just need to offer a glimpse rather than go into a detailed description.

If what you have to offer is obvious, it could just be a matter of literally introducing yourself:

Introducing Harrison's Handmade Furniture.

Or, if your solution requires a bit more elaboration:

Outsourcing part of your manufacturing process will allow you to operate at full capacity without sacrificing quality.

Action IT indicate that they have the answer to the concerns highlighted in the letter's opening by saying:

Well now there's a way to ensure your IT equipment always operates effectively and your data remains secure.

» Introduce an incentive

If there is a special offer, you could introduce that here. Keep it brief, you can elaborate further on into the letter.

Action IT enhance their solution with an introductory deal:

– and it's free for the first month.

Benefits

Now you can detail the benefits of your proposed solution.

By benefits, I don't mean what is so good about your product/service. I mean, how your product/service will improve the life of the customer.

These are two very different things. Customers don't care about how your product is manufactured, how it was developed, where your factory is, at this stage they are not even interested in the product specifications. They just want to know what it can do for them.

As you describe the benefits to the reader of your solution, you should empathise with them. Like Dorothy leading the way along the Yellow Brick Road, give your prospective customers something to dream about as you describe how their life will be changed forever. Use emotion, not hype, so they really feel the benefits as you describe them.

Here are some examples of the very different way businesses see themselves (✗) compared to what they actually mean to their customers (✓):

A personal trainer

- ✗ I can do 200 press-ups
- ✓ I will give you the energy to enjoy your life and make the most of each day

A catering service

- ✗ We bake cakes
- ✓ We transform any occasion into an unforgettable event

An accountant

- ✗ I do tax returns
- ✓ I give you peace of mind and time to do what you do best

And finally, if you haven't already done so, you can drop your company's name into the conversation here, but only in a relevant-to-the-reader kind of way.

Here is how Action IT benefits their customers.

Imagine complete IT support at a fraction of the cost of an IT department. Whether solving technical problems, adding new users to a network or installing a printer, *Action IT* are always on hand to help.

Tailor-made technical services

Whatever the size and nature of your business, *Action IT* offer a bespoke service to suit your individual needs.

☑ IT Management – As well as managing every aspect of your IT network, we ensure your company has full working backups, keep systems up-to-date and provide a rapid response to any difficulties you experience.

☑ IT Implementation – Whether a company-wide network or a PC upgrade, your IT project will be handled with expertise from initial proposal to successful completion and beyond.

Now you can get the very best out of your IT investment. No more downtime, delays, obsolete technology or fear of data loss. And, unlike companies offering a similar service, *Action IT* have no limit on the number of queries, so it really is like dealing with your own IT department.

Note how the use of bullets, subhead, indenting and underlining make it easy to absorb the information. We'll come to that later.

Motivation

You may have presented your customers with the most compelling proposal since Ringo got the call from John, Paul and George – but why should your reader respond now rather than file it away and forget about it?

You need to motivate the reader to take action. This can be accomplished using an offer of some sort, or, if you haven't got one, an artificially created sense of urgency.

» An offer

Your offer, if you have one, has already been touched on. Now is the time to reveal the full details.

 ℓ If it is an amazing offer, you should focus all your attention on that, rather than the product or service. People are much more interested in getting something for free, for example, than the finer details of what it actually is.

 ℓ If your offer is not that amazing, if it could appear a bit of a damp squib on its own, present it as an extra special treat for the reader, like a cherry to top off the trifle of benefits that you have just described.

» An artificially created sense of urgency

There are four ways to add urgency to your letter:

1 Stress that every second counts

So don't let life pass you by any longer.

Don't risk driving without a winter check-up for your car.

2 Emphasise the humiliation of not responding

Your competitors are already...

Your family are depending on...

3 Limit quantity

Only 50 places left.

First 100 calls receive...

4 Limit time

Call before the end of March to...

The enclosed coupon expires...

Action IT use a special offer to motivate their readers:

The FIRST MONTH is FREE if you call now.

```
                    Reassurance
```

Anyone with any intelligence reading a sales letter will be thinking that there must be a catch of some sort. As you are a decent sort that is not in the business of tricking customers, you need to reassure them. Show them there is no hidden trap and your proposal is genuine and mutually beneficial.

You can do this by:

- *Ø* Proving your credentials with testimonials, awards and qualifications

- *Ø* Offering a guarantee that eliminates fear of risk

» Testimonials

Only include genuine testimonials. Customers can spot a fake one a mile away. To give your testimonials credibility, you should include the testifier's full name, business name and web address if appropriate.

To avoid cluttering up your letter and spoiling the flow, you could put your testimonials at the side of the text, or in a separate panel.

Guarantee

A guarantee presents the business as one a customer can trust. However, I would avoid anything with negative connotations, such as a 'Money Back Guarantee' or 'Full Refund'. Instead, present the deal as something more rewarding for the reader, such as a '1-month trial'.

The more specific the terms of your guarantee, the more convincing it is. So be unequivocal and avoid vague assurances, such as 'Satisfaction Guaranteed'.

A car re-spraying service states that:

The finish on your re-sprayed vehicle will look as good as new for one year, or we'll redo it for free.

Action IT allow clients to drop out after their free month, knowing that they will use that month to make the client well aware of the benefits of not doing so:

There's no obligation beyond your first free month, so you have nothing to lose, but a great deal to gain.

What to do

By now, the reader, if they have been targeted well enough, will be thinking, "Yes, this appears to be a perfectly reasonable proposition and I would like to pursue it further," or words to that effect. But how do they go about it?

Often referred to as the Call to Action, this requires more than just a list of contact details, you must literally tell the reader what to do. This isn't a time to be coy, just tell them what to do! If it isn't blatantly obvious, your letter will be like a shop without any discernible entrance.

To give it added impetus, tie your call to action to the special offer or the 'sense of urgency' that you created earlier. Be bold, be explicit, be crystal clear and provide people with as many options for responding as possible.

To get your FREE Demo CD, call... or email...

Complete the pre-addressed FreePost reply card and pop it in the mail.

Action IT simply require prospects to contact them via telephone or email, but they also add the personal touch of the name of the person they will be contacting:

Call me, Ben Wodehouse, now on 12345 123456 or email info@actionIT.net

Summary

A nice neat way to bring proceedings to a close is to summarise the proposition in just a few words. Letters that are longer than one page, require a more substantial summary simply to remind the reader of the key points.

In the case of Action IT's one-page letter, the summary just follows seamlessly on from the call to action:

...and discover how Action IT can provide cost-effective support for your company's IT system.

Sign-off

There are three stages to the letter's closedown procedure: Yours..., Signature and Job title.

Yours...

Presuming your letter is addressed to a person's name ('Dear Mr Collins', for example), sign off using:

Yours sincerely,

If it is not addressed to a person's name ('Dear Sir', for example), sign off using:

Yours faithfully,

» Signature

An elegantly flowing, weighty signature provides the letter with a personal touch – because it has indeed been touched by a person when they signed it. Someone has taken the time to read over their correspondence before picking up their quill, dipping it into the ink well and, with a satisfied smile, signed their name at the foot of the page.

Or so it seems. Depending on how many letters there are, each one can either be signed individually or a signature can be scanned into the computer and inserted into the letter before printing. As long as it looks hand-written and not like a computer-generated font or like a chimp has scrawled it, that's fine. Use a nice pen and take your time, so that your signature is flowing, friendly and legible – and use blue ink to further demonstrate its handwrittenness.

» Job title

Beneath the signature, print the name and job title. If it is from a Sales Manager or similar, the word 'Sales' will instantly undo the camaraderie you have built up and make the reader feel they are being sold to. It is best, therefore, to sign it from the Managing Director.

Action IT's MD signs off like this:

Yours sincerely,

Ben Wodehouse

Ben Wodehouse
Managing Director

Postscript

The trouble with the sign-off that has just been described is that it causes a sudden loss of momentum. It's as if the letter builds and builds, and then drops off a cliff. One way to bounce back before the reader has noticed is to use a P.S. A P.S. is like giving the reader a nudge and saying, "Oh, I forgot to tell you this…"

Now, I know, you've got a computer that can do editing and everything, so why would you need to add an afterthought in the form of a P.S.? Well, as well as re-enthusing the reader before they have had chance to de-enthuse, the P.S. provides another valuable service to the sales letter. For some weird, psychological reason, the P.S. is like another headline. Despite being the last thing on the letter, it's one of the first things people read. Think of your P.S. like that: a headline at the end of the letter.

What should you put in your P.S.? Three basic options are:

- Restate the key benefit
- Restate the special offer or need for urgency
- Restate your call to action

In each case, rather than just repeating the same words that you used earlier, try giving it a twist that roots it in the readers' world and leaves them feeling positive about your solution.

A company installing central heating restates its call to action and special offer like this:

P.S. We get very busy in winter, so call right away for a swift, free, no-obligation consultation before the temperatures drop.

Amazingly, a P.P.S. ranks just about as high in the readers' can't-help-but-read index as a P.S. If you use one, make sure it refers to one of the three options given for the P.S., and

again, don't just give a lacklustre statement, give it a twist
to bring it to life.

> The central heating installers convey the urgency for getting
> a new boiler without even mentioning it directly:
>
> P.P.S. I've enclosed a leaflet listing ways to cut costs on your
> energy bills. As you'll see, there's a great deal of money to be
> saved.

Of course, a postscript is not compulsory, but it is a fact
that they always get read. As long as you have something
worthwhile to say, it is usually worth giving it a go.

> Action IT's postscript reminds the reader of the urgent need
> to act now:
>
> P.S. Did you know that 30% of small businesses go under after
> an IT failure, and a further 50% suffer severe setbacks? Call
> now to make sure your business isn't one of them.

Envelope message

You have just created the most mind blowing sales letter –
and then you seal it up in a plain envelope and pop it in the
post. How is the intended reader supposed to know that it's
even worth opening and not just another piece of worthless
junk?

Here are two options. Which one you choose depends on
how you want your letter to be perceived by the recipient.

1 Put teaser copy on your envelope

Teaser copy is the text printed on an envelope to make the
reader think, 'Mmm, this is worth looking at.' It leaves the
reader in no doubt that there is a sales letter inside, so the
difficulty is coming up with words that entice the reader
rather than giving them an excuse to bin it along with all
the other unsolicited mail.

As with the letter, teaser copy should be benefit-oriented and customer-focused. Think of it like a headline. In fact, you could re-use your letter's headline, or state the special offer, if it's a good one.

In the case of Action IT:

Could your business survive an IT failure?

If there's a free offer inside, say it on the outside:

Gift voucher enclosed

2 Don't put teaser copy on your envelope

If your letter is in a decent quality envelope that is personalised with the recipient's name and address, stamped with real stamps and devoid of your company's name and logo, no teaser copy will be necessary as the envelope clearly evokes integrity.

Putting anything else on the front of the envelope would act as a disincentive, undoing the personalisation by tainting it with blatant commercialism. If practical, you can further personalise the envelope by writing the name and address by hand (neatly, with a good pen).

③ PRESENTATION

The immediate impact of your sales letter is not only determined by the words you use, but also the way they are presented.

To ensure your letter gives the right impression you need to take into account readability, eye-friendliness and the infinite spectrum of sales letter perception.

Put it together

The blocks of text that you have just created are already in the right order (see the illustration, 'What goes where in a sales letter') they just need bringing together. Think of it like a giant game of Tetris.

As the words fall into place, you will notices that some of the text blocks clearly suggest a new paragraph, while others flow naturally together – possibly after a bit of tweaking to smooth the join.

Towards the end of the Action IT letter, the following sequence links together seamlessly in the final paragraph:

Motivation	The FIRST MONTH is FREE if you call now. There's no obligation beyond
Reassurance	your first free month, so you have nothing to lose, but a great deal to gain.
What to do	Call me, Ben Wodehouse, now on 01234 123456 or email info@actionIT.net
Summary	and discover how *Action IT* can provide cost-effective support for your company's IT system.

Edit for non-readers

People don't read sales letters when they receive them, they skim them. Their eyes scan the letter like a what's-in-it-for-me detector, alighting on anything that looks potentially beneficial. If nothing worthwhile is spotted, the letter doesn't get a second chance. This is why you must edit your text to assist skimmers. Like this:

» Break the letter into pieces...

O Subheads - Use between 1 and 3 short, bold subheads to state key benefits.

O Indented paragraphs - You can emphasise an entire paragraph by shunting it in from the left by 1cm or so.

O Bulleted points - Two or three short bullets stand out. Too many looks like a technical document.

» Break the pieces into little bits...

O Short sentences - They get read. Got it? Good.

O Short paragraphs - If a point can't be expressed in a couple of sentences, it is too complex and needs redrafting so that it can.

» Break the little bits up into key words...

O *Italics*, **Bold**, <u>Underline</u>, UPPERCASE, Colour - The occasional word of crucial importance can leap out from a sentence using any one of these highlighting methods. Go easy though: emphasise too many words and nothing stands out.

» Give the words room to breath

O Space - Don't cover every square millimetre of paper in writing. Keep the text minimal and give it plenty of space to stand out and get noticed.

O Margins - Margins of around 3.5cm add more space and ensure the lines of text are not too long.

O Font - Make sure your text is big enough to be easily read by someone without having to fumble for their glasses.

Set the right tone

Although your sales letter should correspond to the layout shown in the illustration, 'What goes where in a sales letter', there is still room for fine-tuning certain aspects of its appearance that significantly affect the way it is perceived by the reader.

For instance, if you wish to give the impression of an en masse, business-like mailing, you should consider a letter with:

- ⊘ A big bold, banner headline
- ⊘ Left-hand-justified paragraphs
- ⊘ A space between each paragraph
- ⊘ Subheads preceding each paragraph
- ⊘ A modern, 'sans serif' font (such as Arial)

If, on the other hand, you wish to give the impression of a more personal, seemingly one-off, correspondence, then consider a letter with:

- ⊘ A gentler-looking headline, grouped to the side of the page
- ⊘ The first line of each paragraph indented
- ⊘ Text written as a continuous flow, with no line-spaces between paragraphs
- ⊘ No subheads
- ⊘ A typewriter font (such as Times)

There is a wide spread of possibilities between these two extremes, as demonstrated by 'The infinite spectrum of sales letter perception'.

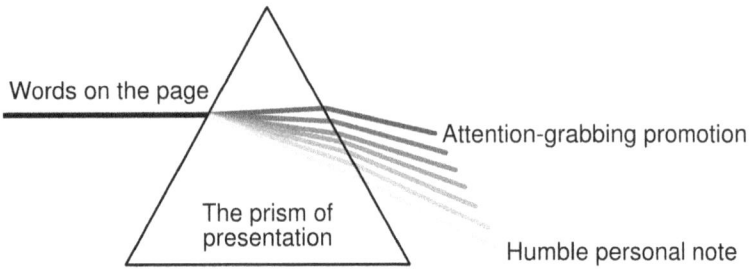

Words on the page

Attention-grabbing promotion

The prism of presentation

Humble personal note

Subtle changes such as those just mentioned will help you position your letter at the point on the spectrum that sets precisely the right tone with your readership.

Here is Action IT's complete sales letter.

Could your business survive an IT failure?

Just because you don't have an IT department doesn't mean you can't have complete IT support

Dear Mrs. Barker,

Nothing wastes time and money in business like computer downtime, especially when there's no IT department to come to the rescue. Well now there's a way to ensure your IT equipment always operates effectively and your data remains secure – and it's free for the first month.

Imagine complete IT support at a fraction of the cost of an IT department. Whether solving technical problems, adding new users to a network or installing a printer, Action IT are always on hand to help.

Tailor-made technical services

Whatever the size and nature of your business, Action IT offer a bespoke service to suit your individual needs.

☑ IT Management – As well as managing every aspect of your IT network, we ensure your company has full working backups, keep systems up-to-date and provide a rapid response to any difficulties you experience.

☑ IT Implementation – Whether a company-wide network or a PC upgrade, your IT project will be handled with expertise from initial proposal to successful completion and beyond.

Now you can get the very best out of your IT investment. No more downtime, delays, obsolete technology or fear of data loss. And, unlike companies offering a similar service, Action IT have no limit on the number of queries, so it really is like dealing with your own IT department.

The FIRST MONTH is FREE if you call now. There's no obligation beyond your first free month, so you have nothing to lose, but a great deal to gain. Call me, Ben Wodehouse, now on 12345 123456 or email info@actionIT.net and discover how Action IT can provide cost-effective support for your company's IT system.

Yours sincerely,

Ben Wodehouse

Ben Wodehouse

Managing Director

P.S. Did you know that 30% of small businesses go under after an IT failure – and a further 50% suffer severe setbacks? Call now to make sure your business isn't one of them.

TWITTER

Build a loyal following, 280
characters at a time

Twitter may not have been devised as a marketing tool, but neither was the telephone or the postal service, and look what a boon they turned out to be.

Like a direct line that lets you interact with real people in real-time, Twitter gives you the opportunity to chat, build relationships and get to know your followers.

But can a social medium be used for marketing without spoiling all the fun? Yes – depending on who your followers are and what you do with them.

WHAT'S IN THIS CHAPTER?

❶ WHATTER?

If you are not au fait with Twitter, if you think tweeting is for birdbrains, or if your general disposition is decidedly anti-Twitter, you may be wondering what all the fuss is about.

Well, read this section and it should clear a few things up. In fact, take a look at it even if you are stridently pro-Twitter. You might learn something new.

Stop the book! I don't know what you're talking about

Here are some quotes[1] from Twitter-sceptics:

"I have absolutely no idea what Twitter is"

Well, Twitter is an online tool for creating short messages (tweets) that can be read by anyone who wants to receive them (followers). Sometimes your followers will want to forward your tweet onto their followers (retweet), and so on, until your original message is being read by everyone on Twitter that is at all interested in what you have to say.

"It's for teenagers and celebs, not business"

According to the evil geniuses behind Twitter, there are over one billion Tweets sent every three days. While you would be right to think that a huge amount of these tweets involve teenagers circulating vital news amongst themselves ('On bus going to shops') and aspiring recording artists subtly promoting themselves ('On bus listening to my awesome new single'), it is also a medium where you can build a network of connections with prospective and existing customers, and anyone else with an interest in your business sector.

---

1 That I have made up

"I haven't got the time for chit chat"

Twitter was originally limited to 140 characters per message, now it's 280 – so brevity is king, whether you like it or not.

If you are wondering what a tweet using all 280 characters looks like, it is precisely as long as this paragraph, including the spaces and full stops. And, because 280 characters is the upper limit, tweets can be as short as you like. In fact, short ones usually have more impact.

"How often would I have to tweet?"

You want to hit the spot somewhere between bombarding your followers and them thinking that you must have died. Tweeting (something worthwhile) 3 or 4 times a week – including weekends – should do the trick, but it can vary depending on what kind of response you are getting.

"I don't want to commit myself to something that I can't keep up"

Twitter does not tie you down. As tweets are so short and can be dispatched and read easily and quickly from a mobile phone, they are perfect for anyone with the occasional observation to share.

"I am too old to understand it"

Tweeting is simple and fun. If you can send a text message, you can use Twitter. If you can't send a text message, it's very easy and you can soon find out from a friend or from your mobile phone's instruction manual. If you do not have a mobile phone, you can use Twitter on your computer. If you do not have a mobile phone or a computer, then… skip this chapter. Life's too short.

"I don't want it to get addicted"

If you have the kind of personality where you just don't know when to stop – use an egg timer, you've got work to do.

"Who would want to follow me?"

Loads of people. But you don't need many. Follow the advice given in this section and give it time. Once you get a bit of traction, things will snowball.

"It's too much of a faff"

There are a plethora of applications (many free) designed to make your Twitter experience a whole lot easier, better and tailored to your needs. Hootsuite™, for example, allows you to schedule tweets in advance. Just get started with the basics first, then see if you need any extra gizmos.

"I don't know how to get started"

Go to twitter.com. Sign up for a Twitter account using your name, email address and a password. That's it. And it's free.

❷ FOLLOWERS

In the non-business world, the success of a Twitter account is determined by the number of followers it attracts. But this is not so with Twitter marketing.

Just as a budding pop star need only send a demo recording to Simon Cowell (or some other major player in the music industry) rather than to every prospective fan, you only need to direct tweets towards the few people that act as a gateway to the wider market.

It is just a matter of identifying the Simon Cowells in your industry and then attracting them to your Twitter account. Do this, and you are on your way to fame and success (and hopefully not dumped as soon as you've had a Christmas number 1).

The right kind of follower

Having lots of followers may make you feel popular, but it won't necessarily help your business.

A taxi firm's wonderfully entertaining tweets were followed by hundreds of people from Preston to Papua New Guinea. As they only served the north Norwich area, however, they were simply wasting their time ingratiating themselves with the wrong people.

Promotional tweets to previous customers may appeal to a few loyalists but will cause mass desertion among the rank and file.

A printer ink cartridge company uses Twitter as well as email and phone calls to hassle every person that has ever bought anything from them since the day they started in business. Their tweets are as welcome as an unsolicited salesman repeatedly turning up at the front door and, not surprisingly, followers rapidly become ex-followers.

Tweets created with specific influential people in mind stand a chance of being passed on. Their credibility and their own following can give a single tweet enormous impact.

Cultivate the right kind of follower
Who reads your tweets is just as important as what you say in them.

The Cakery, a small bakery in Leeds specialising in impressive cupcakes made the effort to cultivate a small number of high quality followers. One of them, an industry blogger whose posts are read by all the bigwigs in food retail, mentions them in a piece about the current craze for cupcakes amongst teenage girls. The following day, the buyer from Marks and Spencer is on the line to The Cakery wanting to discuss those wonderful cupcakes he has been reading about.

At the same time, a presenter from the local TV station who keeps an eye out for local stories on Twitter retweets a Cakery message about 'the ultimate cupcake experience', adding a 'yum yum' comment of her own. It brings in more customers than a mountain of flyers pushed through letter boxes, in a fraction of the time and at no cost at all.

Quality followers trump large numbers of followers every time. Rather than tweeting to anyone that will listen, or pestering potential customers with promotional tweets, the followers that will make a real difference to your business are ones that share a common interest with you – such as location, industry, supply chain or (this is the best one) your target market. A well chosen follower can influence vast swathes of potential customers.

How to get followed (by the right kind of follower)

When you start Tweeting, who is going to receive them? Nobody. Which is why you should put the following methods into practice as soon as you sign up to Twitter. This will not simply attract followers, it will attract the invaluable influential followers that I have just described.

» Write an appealing biography

You are not compelled to submit a personal profile when you sign up to Twitter, but you should. It is how most people find others to follow. Your profile provides you with up to 160 characters to write a potted biography. Forget any ideas about reeling off your life story, it's got to be short, memorable and, crucially, hold out the prospect of there being something in it for the reader.

Here's how to make sure your biography gets noticed by the right people.

Use keywords

There are numerous applications that locate users by searching for keywords in their Twitter profiles. You should, therefore, include keywords that will appeal to your target followers.

A maker of pine furniture in Cardiff specialising in rocking chairs uses the following keywords in their Twitter biography:

Cardiff Pine Carpentry Furniture Rocking chairs

Anyone searching for any of these keywords will find this like-minded tweeter and may decide to take a look at what they are tweeting about.

> TWITTERTIP: Twitter is a social medium and there's nothing more anti-social than blatant search-engine-optimised lists. Keywords should be incorporated into proper sentences.

Describe your business fully

A therapist describes herself as a:

Holistic Therapist providing Health & Wellbeing for Mind, Body & Spirit

You can also use more figurative language to get the message across:

A picture framer conveys zeal for their work with:

The Picture Framer - passionate about art and what surrounds it

Offer something useful

A gardening service tweets daily gardening tips:

Your daily dose of gardening wisdom – from Graham's Gardens

A newspaper photographer tempts followers with:

Behind the scenes tweets from a freelance photo journalist

Keep it punchy

Remember it is not a CV you are writing, so avoid phrases like:

Before being a life coach I was an accountant

Instead write:

Life coach who knows what it's like to be trapped in an office

Express your personality

Although you're using Twitter to market a business, it is still a social medium. So, inject some personality:

> Vicky's Healthfood Store – All tweets guaranteed 100% organic.

Add a website address

Although Twitter does show your web address, you can use your profile to include a useful link to anything:

> When I'm not tweeting or copywriting I write a blog about being a copywriter tiptopcopy.com/blog

Now, put them all together… If you can combine each of these biography guidelines you will end up with a bio that will make you eminently followable by the people that matter.

Here is the completed biography for A Pine Romance, the Cardiff-based manufacturer of rocking chairs:

> A Pine Romance tweets furniture tips & carpentry tricks from their Cardiff showroom while making remarkable rocking chairs. See some at pineromance.co.uk/rocks

» Upload a suitable picture

Another aspect of your personal profile is your picture. As Twitter is about personal connections, a simple smiling headshot works best – ideally with some relevant added interest.

The previously mentioned purveyor of quality cupcakes, The Cakery, uses a snap of the owner taking a big bite out of a wonderful-looking cupcake.

You do see small businesses using their company logo as a picture, but that just makes potential followers feel like the tweets are coming from a faceless corporate call centre.

» Make use of your background

Should a Twitter user wish to know a bit more about you they will click to view you profile page. Only about a third of the screen is used up, leaving a large proportion of the background exposed. You can customise this background to display whatever you want, so you may as well give them an eyeful of something worthwhile: images of what you sell, a shot of someone enjoying your product or service, words offering additional information, or just a lovely picture, nothing to do with your business, just a lovely picture.

» Ask people directly

Of course, enticing followers does not all have to be conducted through the medium of Twitter. You can invite people to follow your business's tweets wherever you encounter them. All they need is the Twitter ID and a good reason to follow you. You should also put the Twitter ID on your business's website and stationary.

» Follow your intended followers

You can view tweets about any business, any brand, anything or anybody mentioned on Twitter. Simply go to twitter.com and enter your search term at the top right of the main page. You can do this without being signed up to Twitter and it is a great way to gather intelligence about your industry, and keep an eye on competitors. You can then choose to follow some of the people that you find tweeting about your industry. When you follow others, they will probably start following you too.

❸ TWEETS

Keeping your followers interested, involves sending them a steady supply of fresh, engaging tweets that they will want to retweet across the Twittersphere and beyond.

While it is true that a poorly constructed tweet can fall as flat as a hedgehog on the M1 and tarnish the image of your business irreparably, there's no need to agonise over every syllable. Just bear in mind the following guidelines and your tweets will reverberate with a resounding roar!

The style guide

If you want to be accepted by other Twitter users and make a success of Twitter's marketing potential, it is essential that all your tweets are…

» Personal

Twitter users are your friends, not customers. So don't be 'corporate'. Stick to your business theme but express yourself with warmth and personality.

» Succinct

Keep it short and snappy. The trick is not to try to say too much in one tweet. Stick to one simple point per tweet.

» Clear

Tweet like you care about what you are saying. Check before you send, removing any sloppy language, jargon, bad grammar or abbreviations that might confuse readers.

» Relevant

Stick to what you do. Your niche is what makes you special and what appeals to your followers. So don't go off-message with tweets about politics or what you had for your lunch.

» No more than 280 characters long

I know, I know. The one thing everyone knows about Twitter is that tweets are 140 characters long. But you may get confused when other things are included (such as retweeted usernames and quotes – discussed later). Recent rule changes from Twitter HQ mean that the only thing that counts toward your character limit is the text you type, nothing else, and as we speak, Twitter is introducing a new limit of 280 characters per tweet.

» Sprinkled with Twitterisms

Give you messages tweet cred (sorry) by deploying these special terms and techniques (see support.twitter.com).

Retweets (RT)

When you receive a tweet that you think your followers would be interested in, you can send it to them by clicking the 'retweet' button and adding your own comments if you wish.

Hashtags (#)

When a word is preceded by a hash symbol (#) it becomes a searchable keyword. This allows every tweet by anyone on Twitter that incorporates that hashtag to be viewed together. It makes your tweet part of a wider discussion. Use the hashtags of events you are attending to become part of that community.

@replies

Clicking the 'Reply' button on a tweet opens up a reply that begins with @username (username of the person you are replying to). This tweet can only be seen by them and any of your followers who are also following them.

@mentions

If you want a normal tweet to be recognised by an individual as directed at them, you can insert an @username (username of the person it relates to) somewhere in the body of the tweet, usually at the end. For example:

Thanks for the mention in your blog @AshHastings

Direct Message (DM)

To send a private tweet to one of your followers, just click on 'Direct Messages' and specify their username.

Put meat in your tweets

Your followers won't appreciate you tweeting just for the sake of it, so don't waste time sending out frivolous fluff. Give them something worth receiving, something that will build your authority, something that they will want to retweet. Something like this...

» Preferential treatment

Offering treats unavailable outside Twitter is a simple way to get followers and spread a positive vibe about your business (especially if the offer can be retweeted).

- *⊘* Notice of price cuts
- *⊘* Special offers
- *⊘* Free online tools
- *⊘* Vouchers that are only available on twitter

Dave's Driving School

I've got 10 half-price driving lesson vouchers. Tell all 17 yr old wannabe Lewis Hamiltons! dds.com/offers

» Hot news

Your news must be of interest to at least one of your followers. If it is clearly a minority interest, then begin it with @username or make it a DM so you are not boring the pants off your other followers. Your news should, of course, relate in some way to whatever you want to raise the profile of:

O New products or services

O Something in your blog

O Something in your website

To pick a completely random example... If someone were to write a terrific book about writing marketing material (ahem) and its details were mentioned in a tweet from the publisher that was picked up and retweeted by The Federation of Small Businesses, all the Local Business Links and Lord Alan Sugar to every marketing person in the land, the author's bank manager would be delighted.

Business Publishing

New book gives every business the marketing skills they need to get their idea off the ground. https://goo.gl/kdowfw

TWITTERTIP: Do not use Twitter for blatant advertising. Any promotion must be part of worthwhile conversation. Otherwise you will be shunned as a spammy fool.

» Inside knowledge

Don't simply tweet what you're doing ('Going to a meeting in Rhyll'), that's not very interesting. Share your expertise or behind-the-scenes gossip to get people hooked on your tweets.

> Tech-know
>
> Just been using Skype with a client - had fun turning on the voice effects. Hilarious! Give it a go.

» Links to good stuff

Use tweets to guide your audience to interesting things that are happening off-Twitter. For example, you could post a link to:

- *Ø* A relevant news article, adding a short comment of your own.

- *Ø* A page on your own website, as long it relates to something worthwhile for the reader. This has the added advantage of boosting your Google rankings as Google incorporates social media links in their search algorithms.

> Spot-On Cleaning
>
> Council puts lots of new jobs out to tender. At last!
> See: EveningPost.com/localgov

A difficulty with this is that web links can be enormous – not leaving sufficient spare characters for you to add your comment. The solution is to tidy up your tweets with URL shorteners, such as tinyurl.com, bitly.com and goo.gl.

> TWITTERTIP: Check that your links work. Otherwise you might be inviting people to check out a big story in your industry that turns out to be a YouTube clip of a kitten.

» Heated debates

Encourage a dialogue by asking questions and inviting opinions. Something not outrageous, related to your area of business and approached sensitively.

Topics can be serious:

Brown's Business Consultancy

How can a small business flourish when it is hamstrung by petty bureaucracy?

or fun:

Brown's Business Consultancy

Was the Business Secretary nodding off during the Prime Minister's speech last night?

Remember, Twitter is a two-way street, so listen and reply to your followers when they tweet back.

> TWITTERTIP: Even the most innocuous opinion can generate unpleasant responses from disagreeable people hiding behind the anonymity of the Internet. Be professional and don't rise to the bait.

» Updates

Keep interested parties aware of last minute changes to any show, event or conference that you are either involved in or share an interest in. As well as being informative, it gives people a motivational nudge.

Altered States Therapies

See you in Brighton tomorrow! #BrightonRocks

WEBSITES

Be loved by search engines and
turn browsers into buyers

As far as websites are concerned, size doesn't matter. Minnows compete on equal terms with whales.

Whether you are Pizza Express or Pete's Café, your site gets exactly the same space on the screen.

The site that succeeds is the one that uses their space best to give visitors, and search engines, what they are looking for.

WHAT'S IN THIS CHAPTER?

❶ WHAT YOU THOUGHT YOU KNEW ABOUT WEBSITES

There is a lot of erroneous preconceived wisdom about websites. So widely held is it that anyone not so familiar with the web could be forgiven for assuming that it must be true.

Before you get started on the content of your website, therefore, it is essential to put the record straight and reveal the truth behind these common misunderstandings.

Mythbusting

MYTH #1: A website is like a market stall

Many company websites shout out corporate hype, branding buzzwords, product features and benefits at the top of their voice like they are trying to attract the attention of passers by.

TRUTH **Visitors come for solutions, not sales**

By the time they reach your website, visitors are already fairly sure you have what they are looking for. The job of your site is to make it instantly and effortlessly available.

MYTH #2: A website is an online brochure

Many websites are presented like pages from a brochure – as though the visitor is expected to sit back with a cup of tea and biscuits while they take a leisurely leaf through the site, tackling each page from top left to bottom right, and not stopping until they reach the 'back cover'.

TRUTH **The online page is nothing like the offline page**

A website does not have the linear progression of a brochure: there are numerous possible entry and exit points; there are hyperlinks that jump the reader to places within and outside the site; and there are competing sites that the reader can leave for in the time it takes to click a mouse. Like serving steak to a customer holding chopsticks, offline literature is great, but it is not compatible with online viewing.

MYTH #3: Readers aren't interested in quality writing

Rather than bother with stimulating prose, many businesses prefer to rely on timeworn phrases: "… in business since 2008 … quality service … exceeding expectations …". Any platitude will do, as long as it fills the space beneath the nice pictures.

TRUTH It is the quality of writing that convinces visitors which site is right site for them

Effective writing speaks personally to the reader. It conveys the information they require with precision and clarity while simultaneously interweaving the company's image, marketing objectives and the unique requirements of the online viewer into crisp, elegant prose.

MYTH #4: People love websites with lots going on

A website with stunning visuals, cool graphics, loads of video, scrolling text, background music and all the latest special effects will impress your friends, your family and your work colleagues – so customers should absolutely love it. Shouldn't they?

TRUTH People love websites that are clear and simple

What customers desperately want is a well-organised website that makes it fantastically simple to find what they are looking for.

MYTH #5: Web designers know what content is best

Many companies abdicate responsibility for their entire website to the web designer. They're the experts, they think, they know what's best, they'll fill my site with good stuff.

TRUTH You create the best content

You know your business and its customers better than anyone, so you should supply the content. Unless you have never given a single thought to what the business is about, you will already have existing material on which to draw as well as ideas gathered from other sources, such as customer questionnaires and competitors' websites. Once you have collated your content, all you need to do is read the rest of this chapter.

❷ STRATEGY

Whether your website is used for e-commerce or public relations, whether it is short and snappy or exhaustive in its detail, it needs to provide visitors with the solution they are looking for – and do so with the single-mindedness of a laser-guided bloodhound with tunnel vision.

Be found

The first step in your site's interaction with a prospective customer is to be found by them. This is more likely to happen if your site appears towards the top of the search results, preferably on the first page, when they carry out a relevant search on Google or one of the other search engines. Boosting your site's findability is called Search Engine Optimisation (SEO).

You might have the best website in the world, but if it is not ranked highly by search engines, you may as well set up shop on the Galapagos Islands.

In ye olde days (about 10 years ago) all SEO involved was repeating popular search terms (keywords) as many times as possible, regardless of whether the text made sense or not. This improved a site's search engine ranking, but made it incomprehensible to anyone who actually visited it.

Nowadays, search engines use complex algorithms that take into account a whole array of sophisticated criteria to ensure the best sites receive the highest ranking. Understanding the criteria they use allows you to ensure your site ticks as many of these boxes as possible.

This chapter confines itself to SEO that can be carried out on the site itself. Look out for the SEO ALERTs given throughout the chapter alongside general advice on content creation. Look, here comes one now.

Your main concern is your customer, not search engines. But you must deploy sufficient SEO techniques to get them to your site in the first place.

Be worthwhile

Once they have found your site, the next step in its interaction with a prospective customer is to offer them something worthwhile.

Too many businesses create a website simply because they feel they should create one. Not surprisingly, this leads to some pretty pointless websites.

For your website to be worthwhile, you must have something worthwhile in mind for it to accomplish.

If your first thought is:

Get visitors

Think again – this may be a necessity for any website, but it does not suggest anything that will excite or engage your online guests.

If your second thought is:

Tell visitors everything about the company, from the detailed workings of each product to the Director's GCSE grades

You lost them at 'Tell'.

When people visit a website they are looking for a solution to a problem. Providing this solution is the purpose of your website.

The 'solution' will also be the key search term used by prospective customers. Optimise your home page for this (keep reading to find out how).

If giving the customer what they want seems too obvious, take a look at a few business websites and you will see that a majority of them cannot resist putting themselves before what the visitor is actually looking for.

What the business wants:

A small metal workshop producing custom-made gates and railings opens with the headline: Welcome to Longbottom Metalworks. Below this is an account of the company's history, workforce, machinery and a brief mention of what they make.

What the customer wants:

Switching the focus to the visitors' needs results in the headline: Custom-made Gates and Railings followed by details of what the customer wants to know: designs, prices, deliver times, ordering process etc.

Establish a clear understanding of what your visitors are looking for. This provides you with a purpose that will shape every aspect of the site and give customers a reason to visit.

> *All visitors want from your site are solutions*
> On each web page, put the solution they seek centre-stage.

Be user-friendly

Once the visitors have arrived at your site, you need to make it as easy as possible for them to get what they came for.

People do not want to plough through lengthy, all-encompassing pages to find what they are looking for. They want it to be instantly apparent.

User-friendly site navigation is achieved by giving every distinct element of your site – every service, every product, every everything – a page of its own, and then making the important pages effortlessly accessible.

Here's how.

1 Know what your customers search for

The terms your prospective customers search for can be figured out partly by using your own judgement and partly by using sites such as

```
adwords.google.com/select/
keywordtoolexternal
```

2 Create a separate page for each key search term

Finer Frames, a picture framing business, organise their pages to correspond with the most popular search terms for their line of work: Bespoke Frames, Ready Made Frames, Temporary Frames, Canvas Frames, Photo Frames, Frame Repairs... and so on.

> **SEO ALERT**
>
> Optimising a dedicated page for a single search term is much more effective than optimising an all-encompassing page for numerous search terms.

Be aware that the words that you use to describe your products and services may not be the same as those used by the customer to search for them.

Finer Frames specialise in a bonding technique called 'non-invasive mounting' that allows an artwork to be removed from its frame without leaving any adhesive residue. However, they know that their customers are more likely to search for the term 'temporary frames'.

3 Prioritise your pages

When a potential customer arrives at your site, they want to see if you have what they are looking for, and that is all.

Think of your website like a drive-thru McDonalds. People don't visit to learn about the company or view one of their advertisements. They go there because they want one of their burgers in their hand as quickly as possible.

There is a time and a place for 'About Us', product features, testimonials and so on, and the main entry pages of your website are not it. Put links to your primary pages upfront and make secondary pages available if needed.

BizMove help businesses with their office removals. Clients typically search for one of three things – Business Relocation, Staff Relocation, IT Relocation – so there are big, clear links to these three primary pages prominently located on the website's home page. A less prominent menu running across the top of the page also gives access to the secondary pages: Storage, Office Clearance, About Us, Quality Assurance, Health & Safety, Environmental Policy.

SEO ALERT

Each page should be no more than one or two clicks away from the home page. Pages buried down a convoluted menu system will be overlooked by the search engines' ranking process.

❸ PRESENTATION

If the words in this book were written in Shakespearean English and presented in the form of a railway timetable, you would be right in feeling that unnecessary obstacles were being placed in the way of your understanding of the text.

The same applies to websites. Readers want a language and layout that lets them assimilate information with effortless ease.

Language

Your website should speak to a visitor as if you were talking to them face-to-face.

Use an appropriate tone of voice. Depending on your audience and what they want from you, they may expect a serious and professional approach, or perhaps they are more interested in building a relaxed and informal rapport. Within these extremes lie many subtle nuances: business-like, friendly, logical, charming, reassuring, straight-talking etc.

 ℰ Don't try to write like something you are not. Just relax and write like you would speak to one of your existing customers.

Show you have the answer to their problem. A client will not feel confident in your ability to solve their problem if you refer to them in general terms and demonstrate no understanding of their business or their circumstances.

 ℰ Make it personal by using 'you' instead of impersonal generalisations, such as 'the client' and 'our customers'.

O Avoid phrases, such as 'whichever business sector you are from', that show you have no personal understanding of the reader.

Remember, it's not about you, it's always about your customers' needs. Even your 'About Us' page (if you have one) is about them.

Layout

Before you can create appropriate content for your website, you need to look through your visitor's eyes...

O They see short pieces of writing

Rather than examining images or ploughing through lengthy paragraphs, viewers eyes tend to rest on stand-alone pieces of text such as headlines, slogans and short summaries.

O They take a shufti

Viewers seldom take in everything that is written on a web page. Unlike in print, where a reader commits to a single newspaper, for example, a multitude of other websites can distract your reader's attention.

O They zoom out from the centre

When they are reading/skimming, they tend to start from the centre of the screen, then glance left and right to see if there is anything worth bothering with.

SEO ALERT: Search engines like to see sufficient text on a page before they will take it seriously. People like as few words as possible. A happy compromise is to aim for 250-350 words per page.

Creating text that fits these and other essential criteria is what the next section is all about.

❹ TEXT

There are a lot of nice looking websites out there, but without high quality strategically written content, they are like a flashy salesman that can't... um... er... whatsit... you know... express himself.

Headlines

The headline is usually the first thing people see when they land on a web page – and it provides them with a should-I-stay-or-should-I-go moment. The entire site may be judged by the first headline the visitor encounters.

Don't panic. This doesn't mean you have to conjure an ingeniously creative headline that will ensnare even the most ambivalent visitor. Remember, most people visiting your website are already interested in what you have got to offer – they just need reassuring they have come to the right place. Clarity is more important than creativity.

An appropriate website headline acts like a signpost that sticks out of the page saying:

The Solution to Your Problem!

Not literally, of course. You need to fill in what solution your product or service provides to the readers' problem.

> SEO ALERT The headline is one of the most worthwhile places to incorporate key search terms. As each page has been based around a specific search term, that should not be difficult.

Using this format, you can produce two different styles of headline:

The No-Nonsense Headline

Combine the problem, the solution and the main keywords into an unambiguous statement that tells visitors in an instant that you have what they are looking for.

Electric City, a team of electricians serving London use this no-nonsense headline on their home page:

Emergency Electrician & Electrical Services, London

The Evocative Headline

Convey the problem, the solution and the keywords in an active statement that brings your solution to life in the mind of the reader.

Electric City highlight their rapid response service on a dedicated page with an imposing image of one of their electricians on a motorbike (with full corporate livery) whizzing past the traffic on a busy London street overlaid with the headline:

Emergency electricians: Not even London traffic stops us getting to you fast

A headline like this evokes an impression of a company the reader can rely on to solve their problem without delay.

A note about the Welcome headline

For whatever reason, the home page of about 90% of business websites use the headline:

Welcome to {company name}

Or, even worse:

Welcome to our website

Do not be tempted to follow suit. The visitor did not pluck your site out from the search engine listings because they wanted to know if they were 'welcome'.

This headline may be suitable for a family's personal website, full of photo's and stories for the wider family to enjoy, but, for a business, it achieves absolutely nothing.

Subheads

After taking in the headline, readers' eyes will flit around the page, and it is upon the subheads that they will initially settle – just momentarily though, so you've got to be quick.

A subhead precedes a chunk of text, highlighting what's so good about it. For every paragraph you write, think how you can express it with impact for a reader with a 1 second attention span. This is your subhead.

SEO ALERT

Subheads, and other prominent pieces of text, carry greater weight with search engines than longer pieces.

Electric City emphasise key benefits as subheads to break up the text:

24-Hour Emergency Call-Out

Free Quote

No Job Too Small

Bullets

The writing on your website is not there to be read so much as absorbed. Rather than describing numerous different points within lengthy paragraphs, therefore, display each point individually as a bulleted list. This turns a piece of prose into something visual that can be assimilated almost as instantly as an image.

1. Use numbered bullets when order is important

• Use plain bullets when order is not important

✓ Keep lists short, 10 items at most

See what I mean?

Paragraphs

When a bullet point is simply not enough and you need to produce a paragraph or two, remember to make each paragraph suitable for a skimmer to glance over.

℘ Focus on what interests the reader. They will not bother reading paragraphs if they are about you.

℘ Make one point per paragraph. Simply convey the facts and key message in as succinct and straightforward a way as possible.

℘ Keep it short and punchy: each uninterrupted chunk of text should be no more than around 50 words.

SEO ALERT Text that is relevant and readable will be ranked higher than meaningless text crammed with keywords. If you have created a page for each core search term, keywords should occur naturally as you write.

Links

Links can take visitors to anywhere within, or beyond, the site. They allow you to provide instant access to detailed explanations, definitions, related content, supporting data... without actually having to pack the current page with it.

> SEO ALERT A link using text that relates to the page it links to, such as 'central heating' or 'custom-made gates', influences SEO more than anonymous statements like 'click here'.

Every page should have links to other pages, structuring your site like a web rather than a collection of discrete documents. As well as menu items and stand-alone links, incorporate links within the flow of your text so that naturally occurring words and phrases link to relevant pages.

Captions

When images, tables or illustrations are used to express something meaningful, an effective caption will summarise the content and accentuate its meaning. Captions can be used to reinforce benefits and reassure readers by tackling possible concerns head on.

Beneath a picture of one of Electric City's professional-looking electricians arriving at the home of a customer in the middle of the night is the caption:

24-hour service you can depend on

Exit strategy

Just as visitors may enter your website at any point, they may exit at any point too. This means that, if they are going to fulfil the objective of the site before they depart – such as buy something, complete a form or get in touch – they need to be able to do it from anywhere within the site's structure. This can be achieved by making the methods of taking action clearly available throughout the site.

There's more to facilitating a response than just making it available, however. You also need a dose of motivation. And this comes in the form of…

The Three Pronged Call to Action

1» What to do

2» How to do it

3» An incentive

An effective call to action includes all three of these elements in a single succinct sentence.

Here are some examples of the Three Pronged Call to Action that seamlessly blend all three elements, moving the reader on towards the desired course of action before they leave the site.

To have it on your desk tomorrow morning, ring this number…

Subscribe now and you will receive…

Submit your details to receive free advice on…

This approach is less presumptuous than hitting the reader with a big phone number and yelling at them to CALL NOW!!! This style of call to action is not only less effective than the Three Pronged alternative, it reflects badly on your company's brand.

Source code

Source code is the computer program that makes your website look and function how it does. This behind-the-scenes techie stuff is not normally something that would concern a copywriter. However, there are some elements of it that are too important to leave to the web designer: Title, Description and Keywords.

If you are unsure what I am talking about, visit one of your competitors' websites and, from your browser's menu, select View Source, and there it is. You can jump to the relevant bits (Title, Description and Keywords) with a 'find'.

Each page has its own source code. So when you give your web designer the content you require for each page, include relevant source code too.

Title

The title provides the wording that appears on the 'headline' of your search engine listing and in the tab at the top of the visitor's browser when they view your page.

> **SEO ALERT** This is a prime spot for keywords. Put your most important ones first. Don't waste valuable characters on your company name, unless it includes keywords.

To maximise the effectiveness of your title:

- Don't just list keywords. Formulate them into a meaningful phrase that will connect with the customer as they scan their search results

- Keep the whole thing under 70 characters long (including spaces). Anything more will go unnoticed

- For clarity, separate phrases with a character such as a bar (|) or a dash (-)

A Cut Above, a manufacturer and retailer of premium wooden chopping boards, has the following title for their 'Bread Boards' page:

Wooden Bread Boards | Quality Boards for Bread & Sandwiches

Description

The description provides the text that appears beneath the headline of your search engine listing. Its primary use is to convince those attracted by the title that yours is the site they need.

> **SEO ALERT** The description gives you a chance to include variations of the keywords used in your title (such as plurals and abbreviations).

To maximise the effectiveness of your description:

- *O* Write in full sentences that will engage potential customers

- *O* Put your site's most popular search terms towards the beginning of your description to catch the eye of people searching for those terms

- *O* Google displays around 160 characters, other search engines display more. So, to avoid your message being cut short, keep it to no more than 160 characters (including spaces)

A Cut Above has the following description for their 'Bread Boards' page:

Solid wood bread boards. Perfect for cutting bread or preparing a sandwich. Handmade from prime hardwoods: Oak, Maple, Walnut, Cherry & Beech. Fast delivery.

Keywords

The Keywords bit of your source code was once considered critical. Now, an absurdly long list of keywords is more likely to have a negative effect as it could be taken as a sign of spam.

Add your list of top keywords here, if not for any serious SEO reason, just for old time's sake.

Other content

Your website provides an opportunity for all kinds of content. This chapter has concentrated mostly on how to write it rather than what it should actually consist of (fair enough, I'm sure you will agree, as you know best what information your business wants to communicate).

You may choose to include material such as case studies and testimonials, as well as product descriptions, blogs and links to Twitter and Facebook (about which you can find heaps of advice elsewhere in this book).

Just be careful not to forget that your visitor has come to your site to get something, and your content should serve the purpose of giving it to them in the easiest way possible.

SUMMARY

When you've got something to say, say it brilliantly

There is a common thread that binds all the chapters of this book together: if you want people to take notice of what you write, you must provide a compelling answer to their fundamental question – *What's in it for me?*

Here, is a concise list of what it takes for a copywriter to satisfactorily answer this question.

Welcome to the end of the book.

If you have read right through from the beginning to the end (well done), you may have noticed that certain themes recur throughout the chapters. I have collated these key principles here in what I pompously call...

The 10 Commandments of Copywriting for Marketing Communications

1 DO YOUR RESEARCH

You can only get to the heart of your subject by exploring it thoroughly and interviewing relevant stakeholders.

2 KNOW YOUR AUDIENCE

When you understand your reader inside out, you can develop your message to harmonise perfectly with their needs, interests and personality.

3 CLARIFY YOUR OBJECTIVE

Without a specific purpose in mind, you are just making small talk. A well-defined objective gives your communications focus and direction.

4 SOLVE A PROBLEM

If you are not improving your reader's life in some way, they are not going to be interested in anything you have to say.

5 GET TO THE POINT

Don't waffle or over-complicate the message. Come right out and say what you have to say. Otherwise readers will lose interest before you get to the good stuff.

6 DON'T WRITE SALES COPY

If you set out to write sales copy, you'll end up sounding like a voice-over from a 1950s commercial. Communicate your message as simply and effectively as possible, and the sales will follow.

7 BE ABSOLUTELY CLEAR

Don't use business lingo just because you're writing business communications. Use simple, natural language, as if writing for a 12 year old.

8 KEEP IT PERSONAL

Imagine you're talking to the reader when you write. Address their needs and say how you can help. Refer to them as 'you', not 'the customer'.

9 WRITE LIKE YOU MEAN IT

Active, explicit language is more important than correct grammar. You're not taking an English examination, you're sharing your passion with real people.

10 SAY WHAT TO DO

You don't simply want people to read what you have written – you want them to act. Give unambiguous instructions on what to do and how to do it.